The Magic Bracelet

TECHNOLOGY AND OFFENDER SUPERVISION

Dick Whitfield worked for over 30 years in the Probation Service, retiring as Chief Probation Officer for Kent in 1999. He is also Vice-Chair of the Howard League for Penal Reform.

He is the editor of *The State of the Prisons—200 years on* (Routledge, 1991) and co-edited, with David Scott, *Paying Back: 20 years of Community Service* (Waterside Press, 1993). His earlier book on the electronic monitoring of offenders, *Tackling the Tag*, was published by Waterside Press in 1997 and he is also the author of the second edition of *Introduction to the Probation Service* (Waterside Press, 1998).

The Magic Bracelet
Technology and Offender Supervision
Dick Whitfield

Published 2001 by
WATERSIDE PRESS
Domum Road
Winchester SO23 9NN
United Kingdom

Telephone or Fax: 01962 855567
E-mail: watersidepress@compuserve.com
Online catalogue and bookstore: www.watersidepress.co.uk

ISBN 1 872 870 17 1

Catalogue-In-Publication Data: A catalogue record for this book can be obtained from the British Library

Printing and binding: Antony Rowe Ltd, Chippenham

Cover design: Waterside Press.

The Magic Bracelet

TECHNOLOGY AND OFFENDER SUPERVISION

Dick Whitfield

WATERSIDE PRESS
WINCHESTER

Acknowledgements

As always, I owe a great deal to the many people involved in electronic monitoring across the world who have cheerfully answered my questions, updated my information and generally helped to piece together the global jigsaw which has emerged. Naming them all would be an impossible task but a special mention ought to go to Ed Mortimer, formerly of the Home Office Research, Development and Statistics Directorate, Stephen Jarvis of the Home Office Electronic Monitoring Unit, Ruud Boelens from The Netherlands, whose sharp and perceptive views always make me stop and think, G David Shellner from the U.S. National Institute of Corrections Information Center and two key figures from the contractors who are currently very much part of the wider scene—Mark Griffiths of On Guard Plus and Andy Homer of Premier Monitoring Services Ltd. Their open, thoughtful, un-partisan approach and their practical experience have been invaluable in trying to put together a realistic appraisal of the wide range of schemes that are now part of the rapidly expanding world of electronic monitoring. Joan Farrall, whose determined work in testing voice recognition as an alternative option is much admired, helped considerably both during the Kent pilot project and in discussion afterwards.

Finally—I always say this and I always mean it—very real thanks are due to Georgie Empson, whose calm, orderly approach and cheerful co-operation makes the production of the final manuscript such a trouble-free process.

Dick Whitfield

May 2001

The Magic Bracelet

CONTENTS

Acronyms and Abbreviations

CSO	community service order
CEP	Conférence Europeaenne de la Probation
em	electronic monitoring
FMD	field monitoring device
GPS	ground position by satellite
HDC	home detention curfew
HDO	home detention order
HMU	home monitoring unit
ISEM	intensive supervision with electronic monitoring (Sweden)
JOM	*Journal of Offender Monitoring*
NCJRS	National Criminal Justice Research Service (USA)
NIJ	National Institute of Justice (USA)
OAS	Office of Alternative Sanctions (USA)
OTA	Offender Tag Association
PDO	periodic detention order
PID	personal identification device
PTD	portable tracking device
RLO	restriction of liberty order (Scotland)

Important note: From April 2001, the names of community orders in England and Wales were altered, to coincide with the start of the new National Probation Service. What was a probation order became a community rehabilitation order (CRO); a community sentence order became a community punishment order (CPO) and a combination order, which combines both of the above, became a community punishment and rehabilitation order (CPRO). The terms are not used in this book since, properly, the earlier titles were all in use when the research and operational work referred to was current. A reminder of the change, however, has been added to the relevant part of the book.

Introduction

When I wrote *Tackling the Tag* (1997) it was never intended to be the last word on the electronic monitoring of offenders. Although the basic equipment had been in use for over a decade in the United States of America, and had established a firm foothold in Europe, it was clear that making effective use of the new technology was a good deal more difficult than establishing its reliability.

It was, in any case, a rapidly moving picture. Basic home curfew systems were becoming more sophisticated, with remote alcohol testing and voice or video recognition as 'optional extras'; there were real advances in satellite tracking, urban location systems using cellular telephone technology and voice recognition as a 'stand alone' alternative where checking at multiple locations was the main requirement in supervising offenders.

My conclusion, then, was that we had reached the point where electronic monitoring had demonstrated its credibility; that it should have a place in the range of options the criminal justice system can deploy and that there was sufficient evidence to show how it could be most positively used. So why, three years later, does it warrant another, wider study?

There are, I think, five reasons for that. First, the sheer scale of the expansion which electronic monitoring is currently experiencing. By mid-2000, over 20 jurisdictions outside North America had pilot projects or established schemes, legislation was being introduced in several others and there is every indication that this level of growth will be sustained for some time yet. Schemes do still vary enormously in size and potential but many are ambitious, and determined to exploit the new technology to the full. South Africa's current proposal to use it for the early release of 30,000 prisoners, over a three year period, is a case in point.

The second reason follows directly from the first. The explosive growth of schemes is driven by a variety of factors—the desperate need to tackle a grossly overcrowded prison population, the search for more cost-effective solutions than prison, the need for politicians to demonstrate that they are actually doing something about crime. Much of this, however, has been without considering the potential long-term effects on community penalties, prison populations and criminal justice policy generally. The impact on sentencing, on public and political attitudes is—mostly—uncharted territory but it needs careful and urgent thought. One aim of this book is to contribute to that debate.

Third, the sheer diversity of current use and practice is badly in need of some dispassionate analysis. Claims of success—and disappointment, as in Canada—need closer examination, too. The capacity of electronic monitoring for misuse; for increasing rather than decreasing prison populations, for expending large sums with little real return—is well known. But longer-term studies are now becoming available and their messages need to be heard.

Fourth, because the ethical and moral issues I wrote about in *Tackling the Tag* have not gone away. If anything, they have sharpened because of technical developments and need to be faced, now. As the capacity for control increases, so does the responsibility for using it fairly and legitimately, especially with vulnerable individuals. The old adage of it offering 'more power than a good man should want—or a bad man should have' is a sharp reminder of the danger.

And finally—because public and political expectations of what it might achieve are still, all too often, wildly unrealistic. What was once described as 'equipment in search of a programme' is in danger of being invested with multiple virtues and being expected to deliver unrealistic results.

I finished my last introduction by noting

> The more sophisticated and powerful the equipment becomes, the more urgent the need to ensure that the enormous potential investment of public money focuses on well thought-out programmes *before* the seductive possibilities of technology blind critical faculties.

Three years on, that has, indeed, become urgent. The ripple effect that expansion has on other areas of criminal justice needs to be explored in tandem. What follows will, I hope, meet that aim.

Dick Whitfield

May 2001

CHAPTER 1

A Short History of Tagging

In practical terms, the electronic monitoring of offenders started in the United States of America in 1984. The concept, and a primitive technology, were being discussed as early as 1919 and there were tentative moves towards commercial use in the 1960s with experiments at Harvard involving students, mental patients and parolees. In the 1980s, however, three factors came together to make development possible on a wider scale—technical advances, a huge and costly rise in prison populations and the growing use of house arrest or curfew schemes.

Home confinement programmes began as a simple way of alleviating prison overcrowding and did not envisage specific treatment aims for the lower-risk offenders involved. Florida's Correctional Reform Act of 1983 defined community control as

> a form of intensive supervised custody in the community, including surveillance on weekends and holidays, administered by officers with restricted caseloads ... an individualised programme in which the freedom of an offender is restricted within the community, house or non-institutional residential placement and specific sanctions are imposed and enforced.

Offenders had to stay in their houses except when working at paid employment to support themselves and their dependants and the conditions were stringent. Apart from the curfew period, which might include the whole weekend as well as evening and overnight periods, there had to be up to 30 contacts each month with the supervising officials, and other requirements which might include community service or fine repayments. The early schemes were quickly hailed as a success and were generally popular with both legislators and the public. More significantly, they were quickly seen to be useful at both ends of the prison continuum—as 'front door' schemes, to avoid the use of prison at all, and as 'back door' schemes, to release selected offenders early in the same way that parole, or licence schemes operate. Either way, expensive prison beds could be saved, it was thought, while keeping the risks of reoffending at a minimum.

Florida experienced a failure rate of around 16 per cent but many of these failures were technical violations of curfew conditions, or failure to pay the monthly fee (another attractive element of the scheme to legislators) rather than revocations for new offences. 'Back-door' schemes tended to have slightly poorer figures—Oklahoma had a successful completion rate of 67 per cent but only five per cent committed new offences, the rest being recalled for absconding, breaking residence or employment conditions, or other programme violations.

The biggest advantage, however, was seen to be in cost terms. A National Institute of Justice (NIJ) report recorded that:

> Since 70 per cent of those 10,000 persons [who had been placed on a variety of house arrest programmes] were believed likely to have been sent to prison otherwise, real cost savings have been released. In Florida it costs about $3 per day to supervise a house arrest offender, compared with $28 per day for imprisonment.
>
> (Petersilia, 1988)

Soon, however it came to be realised that the sheer amount of checking which had to be undertaken by corrections officials would limit the capacity of schemes to a frustratingly low level. An automated, remote checking device which could offer cheap, reliable and large scale checks through computer systems provided the complete answer to this problem and the parallel development of a usable ankle bracelet to complete the system meant that the first continuous home monitoring system could be introduced. (For a description of how the various systems work, see *Appendix*.)

The credit for stimulating development on any commercial scale is normally given to Judge Jack Love of New Mexico's Second Judicial District in Albuquerque. He wanted to divert offenders convicted of drink driving and various white collar offences from the local prison, which he knew was overcrowded, violent and likely to be disproportionately harmful. He apparently approached computer companies, asking them to design a monitoring device after reading a *Spiderman* story in which the villain attached an electronic bracelet to Spiderman, to monitor his movements. The idea was developed and the new signalling device was used for the first time in 1983 on an offender who had breached a probation order. The judge wished to test whether probation could be continued on new and more restrictive terms, rather than go to the immediate sanction of imprisonment. At the same time, a similar system was being tested in Palm Beach, Florida and it was there the first consistent programme started in 1984.

The early years were encouraging, despite a number of technical problems. Within two years of the first Florida scheme, some 30 programmes were in place, with around 1,000 offenders monitored. By 1988 the states of Michigan, Illinois and Florida were all emerging as major users and the average daily tagging caseload was around 3,000. Three years later, Bureau of Justice Statistics reports were logging nearly 400 separate schemes, involving 12,000 offenders. A further boost came with the 1994 Federal Crime Bill, calling for more alternatives to prison and in January 1998 approximately 1,500 programmes existed, with 95,000 electronic monitoring units in use (NIJ, 1999). (This is not the same as the number of offenders supervised—manufacturers' leasing figures were an easier way to measure growth than individual returns from such a wide variety of schemes. An exasperated note in the *Journal of Offender Monitoring* for spring 1998 said, 'On any given day our estimate is that the number of offenders on electronic monitoring ranges from 60,000—75,000. We neither know the exact numbers, nor have the vaguest idea of the impact of electronic monitoring on offender behaviour'.)

What looks, at first sight, to have been a decade of steady growth was, in fact, a rather more chequered period. The early years were plagued by technical difficulties and the literature is full of a vast range of problems which had to be overcome. Transmissions could be blocked or distorted by environmental conditions including proximity to an FM radio station, trailer walls, lightning storms, metal in certain kinds of wallpaper and poor quality telephone lines. Water was also a particular problem—early versions gave offenders shocks when bathing and the discovery that the signal could be blocked by sleeping in a waterbed led to a modest surge in the sales of these partly forgotten items. Power surges and computer breakdowns added to early frustrations and a number of commercial companies disappeared fairly rapidly from the tagging scene.

Schemes also closed for other reasons, including mismanagement, and some simply collapsed under the sheer weight of violations when breaches of the order were so numerous that they could not be followed up. The worst example was in Washington State where, over a four-year period, 7,000 offenders 'went missing' in this way and an FBI investigation had to be ordered. The new (and very competitive) commercial environment was not without a whiff of corruption, either— several states saw officials resign because of commercial links and in Illinois, one who had started a county-run monitoring operation ended by being tagged himself after pleading guilty to four felony counts.

Despite problems, growth continued and it is worth analysing why. First, the operating problems were being resolved, if slowly. Second, politicians were experiencing acute pressure because of an unparalleled growth in prison numbers and budgets. Anything which offered a cheaper option in both capital and revenue terms had to be explored fast.

Perhaps the best example of those pressures comes from Michigan. Perry Johnson, a former Director of Corrections, laid a careful foundation for a comprehensive tagging programme, but at the same time explained the inexorable stresses which led to its growth (Russell and Lilly, 1989).

Faced with an apparently uncontrollable rise in the prison population, the state legislature originally tried to solve the problem through an Emergency Powers Act, which used early release to control the degree of prison overcrowding. When that became unacceptable, the state committed a *billion* dollars (this in a state with a population of just over nine million) to prison building. At one stage it was opening a new prison every nine weeks—only to discover that it would not be enough. With prison operating costs also tripling and beginning to impinge on other budgets, an alternative solution had to be found. (Ironically, there was no parallel 'crime explosion' during this period; the rate and incidence of serious crime was either stable or declining slightly.) A demonstration programme in Washtenaw County led to a state-wide tagging scheme for early release prisoners, which had 800 offenders within 12 months. There was careful selection, described by the Director as a 'blend of common sense, political reality and statistical risk prediction' and an emphasis on employment, mandatory drug testing and caseloads of no more than 35 for supervising officers.

Successful completion rates of over 90 per cent ensured the scheme's growth and the cost benefits were considerable, too:

- cost per imprisoned offender $15,866 p.a.
- cost per tagged offender $4,390 p.a.

Since, as in many American schemes, offenders were required to contribute towards the cost of the equipment used—and did so, on average, by $1,825—the net cost comparison was very much more advantageous.

Interestingly, Perry Johnson argued for a fairly cautious and discriminating approach to further growth, describing its use as appropriate only for 'a significant segment' of the offender group and linked to carefully designed programmes and a scrupulous regard to the early follow-up of violations. He did so because it was already clear that there were wide variations in the ways in which tagging was being used. Many offered simple control and surveillance, with an element of punishment. No attempt was made to do anything other than monitor the curfew hours and the offender's sentence was simply composed of three elements—the restriction of liberty, a degree of stigmatisation and inconvenience through physically wearing the apparatus, and a financial penalty, since many schemes required the offender to pay rental costs for the equipment.

At the other end of the scale, the tag was only used as a component of community supervision programmes, such as probation. Other checks, including regular and random tests for drug or alcohol use were added and groupwork programmes or other elements of intensive supervision were also part of the overall package.

This diversity of aims and methods, together with the very fragmented nature of criminal justice administration in the USA made any detached assessment of the success or otherwise of electronic monitoring a very complex business. The simple, basic questions: who goes on electronic monitoring schemes and who is most likely to do well? what are the success rates? does it represent value for money? and, has it reduced prison populations? all had complex answers. After a decade of use, however, they were not encouraging.

First, it was clear that schemes were concentrating on low-risk, non-violent offenders to such an extent that it was arguable that electronic monitoring could hardly be claimed as an alternative to custody. The characteristics of electronic monitoring participants in a series of studies (quoted in Bonta, Rooney and Capretta, 1999) are given variously as:

- minor, non-violent offenders;
- employed, drink drive offenders attending counselling;
- non violent, no parole violators or offenders showing 'irresponsible behaviour';
- 98 per cent non-violent offenders; and
- limited to those with strong family support.

Defenders of electronic monitoring have argued that the programmes had to begin with low risk offenders to gain public credibility, but the clear and on-going net-widening effect was reinforced by the authoritative summary of research published by the National Institute of Justice in 1994. On tagging, it could only conclude:

> jurisdictions could successfully implement the programs but there were unforeseen technical difficulties ... Further, electronic monitors uncovered many violations which, if responded to, would increase jail and prison costs. On the other hand, low risk offenders (e.g. white collar offenders) were ideal program candidates.
>
> (Travis, 1994, p. 24)

Success rates tend to be measured in one of two different ways - either successful completion of the period tagged or reoffending within a given period following the tagging order. Some interesting evidence is beginning to emerge on the latter, but it is closely linked to the nature of individual schemes and is discussed elsewhere in this book; successful completion of the actual order depends crucially on the period of time tagged. Thus it was relatively easy to achieve a 97 per cent 'success' rate in Florida when the average time tagged was 36 days and the subjects were well motivated drink drivers. The same state, however, was recording a 30 per cent successful completion rate on its Community Control II programme, which dealt with offenders who had already breached other orders and who were tagged for periods of six to eight months.

Over a wide range of programmes, some consistent results emerge, on both sides of the Atlantic. For post-trial programmes, around 90 per cent successful completion seems to be achievable for most offenders where the electronic monitoring component does not exceed two months. For periods not exceeding four months successful completion reduces to about 80 per cent and a further two months' monitoring reduces it again to about 70 per cent. For periods over six months it appears to fall sharply, but the numbers are really too small to quote any benchmark figures.

The question of measuring longer term success by reconviction rates will be dealt with later in this book, and it is clearly likely to be linked to whether the tag is used on a 'stand alone' basis, or in conjunction with other programmes; and whether it was used as a sentence of the court or as an early release mechanism from prison. There is a shortage of longer term studies but in England, Sweden and Canada some interesting findings have emerged. In reconviction terms, the Solicitor General's office in Canada (which commissioned research on schemes in three provinces) was blunt:

> Being placed in an electronic monitoring programme had no appreciable impact on the future criminal behaviour of the offenders. They continued to engage in as much crime as those who remained imprisoned or those who received a sentence of probation.
>
> (Solicitor General, Canada, 1999)

Table 1.1 opposite shows the results obtained from published research so far. It is not intended to cover *all* reported results, but concentrates on the larger and more recent studies. It needs to be treated with some caution because of the wide variety of offenders, order types and variations in overall schemes—and it demonstrates how few follow-up studies there have been. More detailed analysis of some of the recent European and Canadian research can be found in *Chapters 2* and *3*.

In terms of who is most likely to do well on electronic monitoring orders, much remains to be done. Early work in the USA suggested it worked best with offenders

- on a first offence;
- with well established family ties and stable; living arrangements;
- who were not drug or alcohol dependent; and
- who were employed.

This collection of low risk characteristics simply made one wonder if they even needed to be on electronic monitoring orders in the first place—they could equally have been fined, or would probably have done well on any less intrusive community programme. Gradually, though, a picture is building up of the characteristics of offenders who are more likely to respond well to the very structured demands that a curfew order makes, on what can be very chaotic lifestyles. Good targeting of this kind will be a crucial part of successful *and* cost effective schemes.

•   •   •

Table 1.1 Completion and reconviction rates

Study			Offenders	Days tagged	Successful completion %	Reconviction rate %
Ball *et al.*	1988	39	Pre-jail	44	92.3	5.1
		87	Post-jail	55	70.1	3.5
Baumer *et al.*	1993	219	Pre-trial	76	73.1	
		78	Post-conviction	56	80.8	
Maxfield and Baumer	1990	216	Bailees	90<	73.0	
		153	Parolees	90<	81.0	
Beck *et al.*	1990	357	Parolees	126	87.0	
Lilly *et al.*	1992	415	Probationers	48%<30	97.0	11.1
Lilly *et al.*	1993		*Not reported*	76.2	91.3	17.2
Renzema and Skelton	1990	1296	Mixed	79	75.1	
Ontaria	1991	158	Inmates	44	88.0	
Mair and Mortimer	1996	78	Curfewees (1)	101	71.0	
Mortimer and May	1997	375	Curfewees (1)	126	87.0	
Somander (2)	1998	4287	Post-conviction (total)	14	90.0	
				30	83.0	26
				45-60	77.0	After 3 yrs
				91	71.0	
Spaans	1998	330	(87% parolees)	106	90.0	
Canada (2)	1999	262	83 Lowest 37 Highest 140		26.7 (3)	
Begier	1999	3800	Post-conviction	Max. 90	94.0	26 (3 years)
Dodgson *et al.*	2001	1495	Post-release	Max. 60	95.0	30.8 (6 months)
Sugg *et al.*	2001	261	Post-conviction	105 av.	81.0	73 (2 years)

(1) 'Curfewees', because these were a mixture of 'stand-alone' curfew orders and curfew orders made in conjunction with other community penalties, e.g. probation or community service orders

(2) Covers three schemes: Newfoundland, Saskatchewan and British Columbia

(3) One-year follow-up period.

In terms of who is most likely to do well on electronic monitoring orders, much remains to be done. Early work in the USA suggested it worked best with offenders

- on a first offence;
- with well established family ties and stable; living arrangements;
- who were not drug or alcohol dependent; and
- who were employed.

This collection of low risk characteristics simply made one wonder if they even needed to be on electronic monitoring orders in the first place—they could equally have been fined, or would probably have done well on any less intrusive community programme. Gradually, though, a picture is building up of the characteristics of offenders who are more likely to respond well to the very structured demands that a curfew order makes, on what can be very chaotic lifestyles. Good targeting of this kind will be a crucial part of successful *and* cost effective schemes.

While most of the early, and often experimental, work with tagging was undertaken in the USA and Canada there had been other pilot schemes in Britain and Australia before 1990 and a larger and well established scheme in Singapore, where electronic monitoring is used as part of the post-treatment supervision programme for drug addicts.

It was in the mid-1990s, however, that electronic monitoring began to expand to a significant degree outside North America. Teams from Britain, Sweden and the Netherlands all visited the USA at much the same time and all returned ready to implement schemes in their own countries. Despite the common background, however, all three chose to use the tag in rather different ways.

In Sweden it was made clear, right from the start, that tags were never to be used on their own; electronic monitoring only made sense when it was 'embedded in a treatment programme' and even the language reinforced this decision. 'Tagging' and 'electronic monitoring' are never used as descriptions on their own—the phrase used is always 'intensive supervision with electronic monitoring' and this emphasises, neatly, the relative importance the Swedes give the two component parts. The scheme was designed to achieve three main aims:

- to create an effective alternative to imprisonment;
- to reduce its negative effects;
- to reduce the costs of imprisonment

and its success in doing so makes it a rewarding case study, as *Chapter 3* illustrates.

For now, it is simply worth noting that the system in Sweden was particularly suited to an initiative of this kind, simply because there was a pre-existing mechanism which could ensure that 'net widening' did not take place. There, offenders sentenced to imprisonment do not go immediately to prison unless the sentence is a long one or the offence particularly serious. Instead (and especially where the sentence is up to three months) they return home and are subsequently instructed to report to a certain prison on a certain date. This not only prevents overcrowding but enables some flexibility in the process, to take account of individual circumstances. A drink driver, for instance, may opt to use his annual holiday to serve his sentence and so retain his job; a student to finish his exams. It is a practical and humane approach. The gap between sentence and implementation now, however, has a different use.

Courts simply pass the sentence of imprisonment, either because it is mandatory (as with drink driving) or because the offence or offender warrants it. The Probation Service, which operates electronic monitoring, then contacts each offender to ask if they would like, instead, to apply for an intensive supervision period, with electronic monitoring, for the same length of time as the prison sentence imposed. The offender has to meet a number of criteria:

- stay in suitable housing with electricity and a functional telephone;
- be employed or willing to work; or undertaking study or willing to do voluntary work corresponding to at least half-time employment; and
- be willing to participate in a 'personal change' programme arranged by the Probation Service.

It is certainly no soft option—other rules include a prohibition on any alcohol or drugs during the programme (monitored by random testing) and a payment of around £5 per day for use of the equipment (waived where the offender has insufficient means).

Following trials in different geographical regions between 1994-6, the scheme went nationwide on 1 January 1997. Some idea of the scope of the programme can be gauged from the fact that, in its first year of national availability, over 7,000 offenders became eligible; 1,722 did not apply for the new option and of 4,964 who applied, 4,287 (86 per cent) actually started their sentence of intensive supervision with electronic monitoring (Somander, 1998).

The results, from the pilot phase onwards, have been exceptional and make a compelling case for the clear headed, well targeted approach which has been the hallmark of the Swedish scheme.

In complete contrast, England and Wales started in 1995 with a much broader-based, almost 'scatter gun' approach. Legal and cultural differences aside (and they are real, particularly the independence of sentencers) there was also an air of 'never mind the research, or anyone else's experience—we'll let it find its own level' in the way in which it was implemented.

Under the provisions of the Criminal Justice and Public Order Act of 1994, area by area introduction of monitoring was allowed on the following basis:

- the offence need not be imprisonable;
- a curfew order is a community sentence and may be used on its own, or in conjunction with another community penalty (usually, a probation order or a community service order);
- it was available for offenders aged 16 or over; and
- the curfew could be for any period between 2-12 hours per day and for a maximum period of six months.

Three trial areas were chosen and, after a good deal of criticism over the lack of local consultation or guidance, the pilot project got off to a predictably slow start. In the first 12 months just 83 orders were made; thereafter growth was steady rather than remarkable, with 455 orders made by June 1997. As a percentage of the total adults sentenced for the relevant offences, this represented between 1.1 per cent and 1.4 per cent in the trial areas—remarkably similar proportions of the 'sentencing market' to the United States' experience.

The trials continued, with additional areas added, until 1 December 1999, when the scheme went nationwide. By then, however, it was clear that tagging as a sentencing option would be secondary to a new home detention curfew (HDC) scheme, in which eligible prisoners could be released up to 60 days before the end of the custodial part of their sentence. It was for prisoners serving sentences of three months or over, but less than four years—a very large proportion of the prison population. Depending on sentence length, the 'time-tagged' could be between 14-60 days, so this was a very cautious foray into large-scale tagging, with risks properly minimised. In the first year, over 16,000 offenders were released on home detention curfews (about one-third of those actually eligible, so the caution extended to operational selection, as well as to programme design), making this the largest single scheme in the world.

The Netherlands scheme, like that in Sweden, started with the clear belief that electronic monitoring, on its own, had little to offer. It would always be part of a wider programme of activities. The pilot project, which started in July 1995, made it available both to parole (post-prison) cases for periods of between one and six months; and to offenders as a sentence of the court, where sentences of up to one year's imprisonment might have been imposed.

In the event, 80 per cent of the cases in the first three years were post-prison cases, suggesting rather less enthusiasm from the courts than from probation and prison administrators. The results in this period, which saw over 300 participants, were very encouraging, with 90 per cent successful completion and an average of 3.5 months tagged. The Dutch scheme was notable (some thought draconian) for the way in which the curfew was simply part of a 24-hour programme, with very strict limits on social activities and a system in which the right to 'free time' had to be earned over a period.

With a solid foundation laid, it was decided to expand to The Hague at the end of 1998, Amsterdam in 1999 and the whole country by the beginning of 2,000. Ironically, at the time this was decided, the pressure on the prison service had reduced sharply, with some 600 empty cells available (Boelens, 1998) and subsequent growth, especially through the courts, has been rather less than expected.

• • •

With the three major European projects thus established, a flurry of activity throughout the rest of the continent followed. Belgium, Switzerland and Scotland all began small scale projects, with France and Portugal passing the necessary legislation to follow suit shortly afterwards. Germany and Italy will not be far behind.

Elsewhere, similar activity had seen a new scheme in New Zealand and renewed interest and expansion in Australia. But the largest potential development is in South Africa where, as this book was being written, arrangements were being made for competitive tendering for a scheme that would enable 30,000 prisoners to be released early, over a three year period. With prison numbers at 50 per cent over recognised capacity, a 1996 pilot project involving 300 offenders had worked successfully and ministers were prepared to authorise the R56 million project as the only acceptable way to resolve the prison numbers (and cost) problem.

The arithmetic remains as compelling as in the early days of tagging in the USA. South Africa's jails housed 146,000 prisoners in 1999 at a cost of R80 a day; tagging had been costed at R15 a day. With support from organizations like the South African Prisoners' Organization of Human Rights there seemed wide acceptance that, for non-violent offenders it was an overdue solution. One newspaper commented:

> South Africa's jails are horribly overcrowded schools of criminality and violence which are housing 50 per cent more people than they should. This inevitably leads to the brutalisation of inmates, the thriving of prison gangs and the likelihood of graduation to worse crimes … The tag should be a cost effective and humane way of processing (offenders) through South Africa's criminal justice system. Proceed with caution, but do not expect any tolerance from the public for failure.
>
> (*Cape Argus*, 19 August 1999)

The rationale is exactly the same as Judge Love's in 1983—although he wanted to avoid the prison experience altogether, rather than shorten it. It is worth asking, in this short history of tagging, why it had taken almost two decades for the same ideas to be recycled, the same solutions found and the same aims restated? If tagging was the answer to overstretched prison resources, overstretched budgets and was also acceptable to politicians and the public, why had growth been so slow?

There is no single answer to this but I suspect that each of the following had a part to play:

- **unfulfilled expectations**: electronic monitoring was, from the start, oversold. In the competitive scramble for business that characterised the first few years, extravagant claims were made—on reliability and effectiveness in particular—that could not be sustained

- **technical and operating problems:** despite the fact that these have, largely, been resolved they have dogged the industry from the start, with fears particularly centred on the ability of offenders to circumvent the system. As recently as 1998, one respected expert was writing:

  The successful circumvention of tamper technology is a hard fact for most agencies or manufacturers to swallow. But it cannot be ignored. (Conway, 1998)

  The proportion of cases where this happens is probably tiny. Claiming it does not, weakens confidence considerably.

- **mixed outcomes**: with few exceptions (Sweden being the most obvious) electronic monitoring has simply not delivered its original promise—to reduce prison populations. The fact that it has failed is not the fault of system manufacturers or operators—it lies with selection for the schemes, political and agency caution in keeping it to low risk offenders, and automatic violation penalties. The latter, often devised with reassurance of the public in mind, have often been a prime cause of net widening. The fact that, internationally, the balance towards post-prison tagging is shifting considerably is a recognition of how difficult it is to 'get it right' when used as a sentence. The rewards, both financially and otherwise, are greater, since prison does not have to be used at all. But post-prison schemes *do* have economic advantages in releasing expensive prison beds early and, though it may be a lesser gain, they have a generally good track record. I estimate that in 1995 only 20 per cent of electronic monitoring cases were 'back door', or early release schemes. By 2002 that proportion is likely to be around 60 per cent—and growing.

- **slow learning:** the very diverse and fragmented nature of the criminal justice scene in the USA makes learning from research difficult. So much of the early literature is on small scale, pilot projects that drawing wider conclusions would hardly have been justified. The USA has, rightly, been described as 'the penal laboratory of the world' but it is a laboratory where the good, the incompetent, the bizarre and the indifferent all seem to flourish equally. The alternative view of the country as the world's first free range lunatic asylum has meant that much useful experience has been discounted or ignored.

While growth outside the USA has been slow and cautious, it has also disappointed within that country. The specialist journal that covers developments and research, as well as conducting an annual survey of the industry is the authoritative *Journal of Offender Monitoring (JOM)*. Yet by spring 1999 it was discussing an 'electronic ceiling' which it was assumed was inhibiting growth (to around 100,000 units in the USA) and which would have to be overcome if the industry were to move forward. It believed three factors had to be addressed: proper development as a community based penalty rather than just a quick fix for prison overcrowding, much better evaluation of schemes (especially outcomes); and the lack of any national organization in the use of electronic monitoring. For an industry with such an impressive record of technical innovation it was—and remains—a very downbeat view.

At the end of the 1990s it became clear that electronic monitoring was going to become more diverse, with a range of options rather than the concentration on home monitoring systems. They, in turn, were becoming more sophisticated, with remote drug and alcohol test facilities built in to some systems. But it was the potential to track offenders' movements, rather than just monitor a static location that excited most interest. Satellite tracking using GPS systems (ground position by satellite) had been commercially available for yachts, earthmovers and a wide range of vehicles for some years. But problems of battery size and weight, signal interference, cost and complexity had limited operational experience and there was a growing recognition that it was only likely to be used for the most serious offenders. Alternative methods of tracking movement through cell-phone technology and smaller scale urban locator systems were also being explored. (For a more detailed explanation, see *Appendix*.)

Another interesting variation was the use of computer-aided voice verification, in which both an identity check and a location check (from the land-line telephone) could be carried out swiftly and cheaply. The system did not provide continuous home curfew monitoring, like the bulk of tagging schemes, but could be used flexibly (from a range of agreed telephone numbers) as a useful adjunct to supervision. The company with most experience in this field, Voice Track, already had experience of monitoring 7,000 offenders in this way when the Home Office funded the first European experiment, run by Kent Probation Service.

To conclude this brief history of tagging, the important messages are as follows:

- electronic monitoring products for home curfew schemes have matured, and work reliably. Growth has been inhibited by poor selection and targeting but we now have a much better idea of what works and with whom;

- a broader range of technologies and solutions is rapidly becoming available for more sophisticated checks on selected offenders. Even though they can be three or four times as expensive as basic home monitoring, the economic case (compared with the cost of prisons) remains compelling; and

- electronic monitoring has a variety of uses—as a condition of bail, as a community penalty and as an early release mechanism from prison. All can contribute quite significantly at different stages of the criminal justice process. Just how large that contribution will become depends on a number of factors, including public confidence.

This, then, is the background to this current study. What follows is a description of current use and developments in Europe, North America and the rest of the world; a discussion of its impact on sentencing, especially with juvenile and young adult offenders; a review of the wider issues which electronic monitoring raises; research results and a look to the future.

REFERENCES for *Chapter 1*

Boelens R, 'Electronic Monitoring in the Netherlands: an Overview', Conference Paper, London, ISTD, 1998

Bonta J, Capretta SW and Rooney J, 'Electronic Monitoring in Canada', Canada, Solicitor General's Office, May 1999

Conway P, 'Technology—it's Time for the Truth', *Journal of Offender Monitoring*, Vol. 11, No. 3, pp. 25-6, Kingston N.J. 1998

NIJ, 'Keeping Track of Electronic Monitoring', *National Law Enforcement and Corrections Technology Centre Bulletin*, Rockville MD, October 1999

Petersilia, J, 'House Arrest', *NIJ Crime File* 104559, Rockville MD, 1988

Russell K and Lilly R (Eds), *The Electronic Monitoring of Offenders*, Leicester, Leicester Polytechnic Law School, 1989

Solicitor General, Canada, *Research Summary Bulletin*, Vol. 4, No. 3, Ontario, Canada, May 1999

Somander, L, 'The First Year of Nationwide Intensive Supervision with Electronic Monitoring', *Kriminalvården*, Norrkoping, 1998

Travis, J, 'Twenty-Five Years of Criminal Justice Research', Washington DC, NIJ 151287, 1994

CHAPTER 2

Current Use and Development: the UK

Electronic monitoring in the UK has had four distinct phases—the use of curfew orders as a sentence of the court, home detention curfews as an early release scheme from prison, alternative uses for tagging in England and Wales (bail and as an alternative penalty for fine default and petty persistent offending) and the Scottish system of restriction of liberty orders. All these will be considered separately, as will the trials of voice verification systems, which offer an interesting option in terms of different usage and flexibility.

First, however, it may be useful to provide an introduction and brief chronology, so that it can be seen where the pieces of this increasingly complex jigsaw fit together. The key dates are as follows:

- **1989:** First bail experiment
- **1995:** Curfew orders pilot project in three areas (Norfolk, Reading and the City of Manchester)
- **1997:** Trials extended to Cambridgeshire, Middlesex, Suffolk and West Yorkshire
- **1998:** Scottish pilot project on restriction of liberty orders begins;
  - trials begin in Manchester and Norfolk for use with petty persistent offenders, fine defaulters and with ten to 15-year-old offenders;
  - trials begin in Norwich and Manchester to use electronic monitoring to enforce conditions of bail;
  - voice verification pilot project starts in Kent
- **1999:** January—home detention curfew scheme introduced in England and Wales;
  - December—curfew orders become available to courts across the whole of England and Wales.

Development has, as this timetable shows, been very rapid and once a national infrastructure was available there was no reason not to make the best possible use of it. Progress has, however, not been as smooth as that record of expansion would seem to indicate and there are certainly lessons to be learned, both from the way in which it was introduced and in terms of criminal justice initiatives generally.

The House of Commons Home Affairs Committee suggested in 1987 that electronic monitoring 'might be helpful in connection with supervision orders' but this was not the first time the idea had surfaced.

Tom Stacey, a novelist and film maker who had earlier been jailed in the course of his work as a journalist, took the idea to the Home Office in 1981. But his proposals for a feasibility study in conjunction with the University of Kent's electronics laboratory were turned down and although he formed the Offender Tag Association (OTA) in 1982 and campaigned hard, little was done until the suggestion to study progress was made by the Home Affairs Committee, five years later.

Having determined to experiment with electronic monitoring, the government let it be known that it was considering a wide range of options—in relation to bail cases, as part of community sentencing 'packages' so that it would be an alternative to a prison sentence and as a way of strengthening parole supervision, post-release. There was vocal opposition from most sections of the criminal justice process, and from reform and pressure groups, but—interestingly—readers of the *Sun* newspaper were rather more positive. In a poll (2 May 1988) only 15 per cent of its respondents were in favour of more prisons, but a significant majority were in favour of tagging.

The go-ahead for trials was announced in October 1988 but it was the following August before the first of the three pilot projects began in Nottingham. North Tyneside and Tower Bridge court, in London, followed within the next two months. The objectives for the trial were clearly set out—to evaluate the usefulness of electronic monitoring for offenders on bail, including the technology, cost effectiveness and the use of the private sector in such schemes; and 'to inform consideration of the scope for widening the application of electronic monitoring to convicted offenders who would otherwise have received a custodial sentence' (Grant, 1989).

The aims were realistic enough and had they been met there was sufficient political and Civil Service support to mount a rapid expansion of the scheme. Instead, the pilots veered between failure and farce from a very early stage and were followed by a six-year gap before another cautious start was made. The Home Office had expected that at least 150 offenders would be tagged in a six-month period—a not unreasonable hope, given that the three courts remanded, between them, over 1,000 defendants to prison each year. In the event, just 50 orders were made before a decision to halt the trial was taken at the end of January 1990. Of those, eleven had reoffended whilst being monitored and 18 had violated bail conditions in other ways. The trials had resulted in a failure rate of 58 per cent and, because of low numbers, cost about £14,000 per monitored offender. It was an inauspicious start.

During the trial period, there was a steady stream of stories for a rather gleeful press, too. The first tagged offender, a somewhat restless sleeper, was to suffer no fewer than 15 night visits during his bail period because the equipment registered that he had left home. Yet each time, 'he was still beneath the duvet, having a restless night' as one newspaper recorded. The third defendant simply removed the tag and absconded, only ten minutes after returning home; another absconded and, when found, was charged with murder, for which he later received a life sentence.

Ministers put on a brave face—there was certainly enough evidence elsewhere that tagging *could* be made to work—and maintained that, when equipment improved and the time was right, a second attempt would be made. Legislative provision was made in the Criminal Justice Act of 1991, and then the Criminal Justice and Public Order Act of 1994. This enabled the curfew order to be introduced as a community sentence in its own right, or as an adjunct to any other community penalty.

By the time the new pilot project began in July 1995, the criminal justice climate had altered significantly. The two main political parties were competing to see whose 'tough on crime' credentials could be presented most convincingly; 'Prison works!' had become the then Home Secretary's rallying cry and the notion that tagging's main role might be as an alternative to a more damaging prison sentence was quietly shelved—in public, at least. Instead, as one detailed study (Paskell, 1999) records, punishment was presented as the main purpose. This was a tough, swiftly enforced penalty to restrict offenders' liberty, provide a constant reminder of the requirements of the court and to supply an additional punishment to community sentences such as probation or community service, which were seen to be 'too soft'.

Punishment, control and surveillance were the key words in introducing this new option for the courts—but, of course, although not designed to tackle offending behaviour, it was always clear that its impact would also be measured in reoffending terms. Indeed, the Home Office approach, which made it available very widely, either as a sentence in its own right, or as an additional penalty when probation or community service was being used, allowed researchers to measure, differentially, the impact it seemed to have in different situations.

All this was in total contrast to Sweden and the Netherlands, whose officials had travelled to the USA at the same time as their English counterparts to examine tagging schemes at first hand; had looked at the same research evidence—and come to completely different conclusions. Electronic monitoring, they both decided, had no future unless it was 'embedded in a treatment programme'. On its own, it offered little in terms of public protection, still less in terms of reducing offending behaviour. Both countries introduced it as a component part of intensive probation programmes, designed specifically to reduce prison numbers. It meant that the British experience—starting with the 'scatter gun' approach in England and Wales, then the more closely targeted pilot project in Scotland—would be under very close scrutiny to see whether it could demonstrate a more central place for tagging in the sentencing armoury. How it fared is best described, and assessed, in the separate categories listed at the head of this chapter.

CURFEW ORDERS AS A SENTENCE OF THE COURT

Three areas were chosen for the initial trials—the county of Norfolk, the city of Manchester, and Reading in Berkshire. The idea was to have three very different experiences—one, predominantly rural and sparsely populated, the second densely populated and with inner city characteristics and the third, a medium sized town in Britain's high-tech 'silicon valley'.

The trials got off to a poor and sometimes bizarre start, however. There were criticisms of lack of consultation with sentencers and local probation services (both of whom were key to the project's success) and a complete lack of guidance as to what the new sentence was designed to achieve, and for whom. Home Office officials countered this by pointing out that they do not offer guidance on sentencing, which is properly a matter for the courts. But there is little doubt that some shared clarity over aims and objectives at an early stage—which could certainly have been undertaken without undermining the independence of the courts— would have helped the first year of the trials considerably.

Home Office Ministers and officials were also critical about what they saw as opposition and obstruction from probation officers in the early stages of the trials. Some of this, from individual officers, was undoubtedly ideological, but for most it sprang from confusion. Here was yet another option to be covered in pre-sentence reports, but guidance on targeting was lacking and, although many could see how it might be used in terms of reducing the opportunities for offending, there were two unanswered fears. Would it, as seemed to be the case in the USA, simply hasten the path to prison for minor offenders, because of breach action? And would it, as USA reports also made clear, simply drain cases and resources from mainstream probation?

It was also unfortunate that the very first, well-publicised, use of the tag seemed set to repeat the comedy of errors that had dogged the earlier bail experiment. Magistrates in Kings Lynn (Norfolk) made the order on a man later described as 'a publicity-seeking, serial shoplifter'. The 46 breaches of his curfew order in the first few weeks did at least demonstrate that the monitoring equipment worked—although, as the company's representative wryly pointed out, it would hardly have mattered if it didn't, since there were so many reporters camped outside the house, keen to report the latest infraction. Meanwhile, the offender could be found offering to pose for pictures, wearing his tag, in return for £300, and giving interviews to any reporter who would listen.

After only four months the trial area was almost doubled, but after 12 months just 83 orders had been made. The successful completion rate was over 80 per cent but this, of course, included those who had breached the conditions of the order and been returned to court, but had been allowed to continue. It was a disappointing start and much too small for any reliable data to emerge. Yet the criteria were as wide as they could have been. Curfew orders were available for:

- any offence for which the offence was not fixed by law;
- all offenders aged 16 or over (ten per cent of orders in the first year were made on 16- or 17-year-old juveniles); and
- wide curfew differences existed of between two and 12 hours per day for periods of up to six months (designed to cover 'periodic' offenders such as football hooligans as well as more persistent offenders);

with the only restrictions that the orders should, as far as possible, avoid conflicting with school or work attendance, religious beliefs or the requirements of other community orders. Section 6 of the 1991 Act also reinforced the fact that they could be used as a 'stand-alone' penalty or in combination with other community orders.

By this time a new government had been elected but the new Home Secretary, Jack Straw, made it clear that tagging remained firmly on the agenda. He said:

the three pilot areas will each be extended (a second time) to neighbouring counties to cover at least twice the population. I shall also be piloting tagging to cover those on bail as well as for fine defaulters, petty persistent offenders and 'juveniles'.

(Parliamentary Statement, 30 July 1997)

If tagging was to become an all purpose option, however, it was still a long way from general acceptance. After two years of high profile development, only 110 orders were being supervised at any one time. The key figures were the percentage of tagging orders made for relevant offences in the pilot courts, over the period. They were:

Greater Manchester	1.4 per cent
Norfolk	1.3 per cent
Berkshire	1.1 per cent

The figure was very comparable to the American experience, with tagging achieving a 1.5 per cent 'market share' within the wider criminal justice process, after a decade of use.

The scheme had, however, been well researched from the beginning and two reports (Mair and Mortimer, 1996; Mortimer and May, 1997) from which the following figures are taken, allowed some interim judgements to be made. A total of 443 curfew orders were considered:

- 313 were completed successfully without breach;
- 46 were breached but allowed to continue and were later completed satisfactorily;
- 3 were revoked for non breach reasons; and
- 81 were revoked following breach proceedings

from which the 82 per cent successful completion rate was derived.

There were significant differences between two of the project areas—Norfolk had a 91 per cent successful completion rate compared with 79 per cent in Manchester—but these were explained by differences in the type of orders made. Norfolk had a higher proportion of Crown Court orders, which had a 97 per cent success rate; Greater Manchester had far more Youth Court orders which, like most other Youth Court orders, were more volatile, with a success rate of 68 per cent. Completion rates also varied by main offence, as *Table 2.1* shows.

Numbers may be too small to start drawing any definite conclusions yet, and in any case reconviction research will show whether there has been any impact on reoffending rates. But experience is beginning to crystallise views on who might be most suitable. Three-quarters of sentencers and probation staff (in Mortimer, Pereira and Walter's study) suggested certain types of offenders or situations in which tagging might be appropriate:

- as a high tariff sentence for serious offenders where custody is a possibility;
- to disrupt 'pattern offending' e.g. shoplifting, night-time burglary, public order offences on a Friday and Saturday night; and
- where extra punishment is called for.

There were more conflicting views on drug misusers (where the Norfolk trials did show some real success in bringing some discipline and constraints into otherwise chaotic lives) and with young offenders (where probation officers stressed the need for a stable home life if tagging were to be effectively used).

Table 2.1 **Home detention curfew completion rates**

Offence type	Valid cases	Per cent complete
Violence	51	78
Burglary	77	74
Theft and Handling	129	77
Drugs	13	92
Dishonesty	14	100
Criminal Damage	12	100
Taking m/v w/o consent	31	74
Driving while disqual.	64	91
Drink driving	21	95

(Mortimer *et al.*, 1999)

Offenders are much more difficult to categorise than offences. But I think there are some characteristics which make individuals more likely to respond positively to tagging and, over the last three years, I have collected information from supervising officers on both sides of the Atlantic to see if a typology could be developed, to help in the assessment process. Since I first—and rather tentatively—made it public, I have been encouraged by the number of staff who say they have used it, and done so successfully. It needs more work, and rather more rigorous definitions, but the following characteristics seem to be important; apart from the obvious group of offenders where time and place are crucial to offending patterns and may therefore be controlled by a curfew order—they are:

(1) *People who need help in dealing with authority figures*
 The 'authority' of the tag is wholly impersonal. Accepting it involves no personality clashes, no loss of face. Many tagged offenders test out the boundaries in an order, very quickly. Most accept, surprisingly quickly, that there is nothing personal in its swift response; many invest rather more power in the technology than it actually has. High compliance rates are the positive outcome.

(2) *People who need help to resist peer pressure*
 Young adults, in particular, frequently commit offences in groups and the fear of backing down, losing face and peer pressure generally drag many young men into group offending from which they would prefer to keep clear. The young 'twoccer' who told me that the tag was the perfect excuse for keeping clear of his mates (who were continuing to take cars) because 'you can't fool the tag' was typical of this group.

(3) People who need a reason to change

A similar, but less specific group, whose resolve to stop offending (always given with real sincerity at the pre-sentence report stage) needs some practical support as time goes on. Offenders' partners, in particular, seem to make positive use of this—they know instinctively what research has often told us—that for persistent and prolific offenders the first significant gap in offending behaviour—even if only three or six months—may be crucial in building longer offence-free periods later.

(4) People who need a success to build on

It is a long time before a probation order can be judged a success; each curfew period successfully met, however, is a small success of a type some offenders badly need. In the early pilot schemes, when numbers were low, some contractors' staff did use a very successful 'positive reinforcement' technique to ring offenders at the end of a day, a week, or a month to boost confidence in an offender's ability to complete successfully.

(5) People who have breached a community order but have still made considerable progress

Probation officers have, traditionally, used a good deal of discretion in deciding whether to jeopardise a whole order because of a minor or 'one off' breach of a more serious nature. That discretion has been reduced considerably in recent years and courts are now having to deal with many more breach proceedings. They pose many difficulties—a lesser response may be seen as 'getting away with it'; a harsher one may jeopardise months of hard-won progress in offending behaviour work. Tagging simply offers courts another useful option. A degree of punishment can recognise the seriousness of the breach without disrupting any longer term and more positive work.

(Whitfield, 1999)

The Home Office is undertaking further evaluation work on the national picture, reconviction studies and parallel evaluation of the Home detention curfew scheme, so good quality research information should soon be able to produce a more definite picture.

There was more agreement on cases where tagging was felt to be unsuitable:

- where there are risks to the family or public e.g. domestic violence;
- where there are child protection issues;
- where the offender has physical or mental health problems;

- where there are specific family considerations for carers, mothers or pregnant women;
- where the order was unlikely to succeed; and
- where offenders are substance misusers and/or have chaotic lifestyles.

However this last group—perhaps the last two groups—are arguable, especially given experience from the early trials.

A good deal of interest was focused on whether 'stand-alone' orders would fare less well than offenders on orders in which the tag was combined with a treatment programme (on probation) or with some other penalty like community service. Experience elsewhere certainly suggested that this would be the case, and it is why both Sweden and the Netherlands decided they would only use electronic monitoring in conjunction with another programme.

In the event, the two-year research has not yet cleared this up.

Forty-five per cent of the orders examined were 'stand-alone' and the completion rates for the three categories were:

Joint orders	143 cases	77% successful completion
Pre-existing sentence *	99 cases	80% successful completion
Stand-alone orders	201 cases	86% successful completion

(* Pre-existing orders were where another community penalty was already in force when the curfew order was made.)

The figures may be misleading, however, since stand-alone orders were more likely to be made in respect of lower seriousness offences—assault, public order and drive whilst disqualified—where custody would have been unlikely. This contrasts with burglary cases, 45 per cent of which resulted in a prison sentence in 1998, where a joint order was usually made. More work is certainly needed in this area since, if only one intervention is really needed, why waste resources on more?

The question of whether tagging's role in the sentencing 'tariff' was really as an alternative to custody remains open. Twelve per cent of those in the study had no previous convictions—but nine per cent had at least 20 previous convictions. This is not necessarily the only indicator of a custodial sentence, but it does demonstrate the wide range of usage. The first year study was properly cautious; it said

> . . . over half of all offenders tagged had previously served a custodial sentence. While this should not be interpreted as unequivocal evidence that electronic monitoring is being used as an alternative to custody, it does at least point in that direction.

> (Mair and Mortimer, 1996)

The second year study, equally properly, did not go that far—but we need to have a view, as the scheme expands, if we are to make judgements on cost effectiveness. We also need to judge whether (as in so many schemes in the USA) all tagging has done is increase the scale of intervention into offenders lives without commensurate benefits.

One very clear result has been the link between successful completion and the length of time tagged, as *Table 2.2* shows.

Table 2.2

Length of Order	No. completed	Successful completion
up to 1 month	12	100%
1-2 months	74	95%
2-3 months	118	84%
3-4 months	53	79%
4-5 months	14	67%
5-6 months	29	64%

(Mortimer and May, 1997)

This confirms both international experience and first year experience of the much larger home detention curfew scheme here. Tagging works best as a short term alternative. It works best of all if both that, and careful targeting, are taken into account.

The national 'roll out' of curfew orders, which made them available to every court in England and Wales, took place on 1 December 1999. By then over 3,000 orders had been made, over four years, in the extended trial areas and an overall successful completion rate of 82 per cent was seen as providing everyone—from politicians to practitioners—with the confidence to go ahead.

The Home Office's 'Information for Sentencers' spelt out clearly the respective roles of the contractors and probation service staff; explained the electronic monitoring process; defined violations and breaches and enforcement procedures; and summarised existing research. But it remained reticent in the face of magistrates' most common question—whom is it best used for? It simply included the following comments:

Ministers believe that curfew orders controlled by electronic monitoring can potentially achieve four aims. They can:

- restrict liberty in a systematic, controlled way;
- make it harder for the offender to commit further crimes;
- interrupt the pattern of offending; and
- provide clear evidence of curfew compliance.

It added that curfew orders (in the pilot areas) 'were *seen as* an alternative to custody and at the higher end of community penalties'. There was also a cautionary note:

> Electronic monitoring is very effective in its defined usage. It is not, however, suitable for everyone or in all circumstances. It cannot prevent offenders from breaching their curfew, or committing further offences, nor does it record details of further offences being committed ... It simply records whether the offender is at the specified place during the hours specified by the court and whether or not they are complying with the terms of the curfew.

> (Home Office (1), 1999)

I spent some time talking to magistrates that autumn about their new sentencing option—and found them puzzled, if not exasperated, by the lack of guidance. 'Of course, we make the decision in individual cases' said one 'but if, after 3,000 orders they can't tell us who it works best for, how are we going to decide? We might only see one potential case a month.'

Results so far suggest that view was shared by many others. After weighing up the experience from the extended trial areas, the Home Office told probation areas that the projected number of curfew orders to plan for was 10,000 in the year 2000, rising to 12,000 in 2001 and 2002 (Home Office(2), 1999). In fact, the figure for 2000 is expected to be just over 4,000—less than half the original estimate. What is apparent is how varied usage is between different courts (an almost inevitable result, given the wide variety of sentencing options available) and that, once established in a local bench 'culture', then regular usage does start to occur. It suggests that, while growth is slow, it does seem likely that tagging will soon become a significant option, alongside other community penalties.

Quite apart from numbers, however, Home Office researchers also wanted to find out whether a consensus was emerging in relation to suitability, the use of joint and stand-alone orders, breach proceedings and the perceived advantages and disadvantages of the sentence. With this in mind, interviews were conducted with both criminal justice practitioners and staff from the electronic monitoring companies.

The results (Walter *et al.*, 2001) reinforce many of the messages which were already apparent. Most saw curfew orders as a 'top end' community penalty, but recognised that its flexibility could lead to wider and perhaps more imaginative use. More specifically, its value for 'pattern' offending which occurs at specific times or places was recognised; it could be proposed where custody was likely but inadvisable and could also be used when other community penalties had been breached or were unsuitable. Most felt curfew orders were inappropriate for sex offenders or very violent offenders, but opinions were much more divided where substance abusers and more chaotic offenders were concerned.

With these positive views of the order, why had take up been so slow? Practitioners felt inundated by new initiatives and were inhibited by lack of knowledge about and confidence in the order. The latter problem was also affected by what were seen as inconsistent approaches by courts to breaches. This was particularly the case where a curfew order had been given jointly with another community penalty, with which the offender was complying. Sentencers were unclear whether one or both parts of such orders should be revoked and on what basis they should resentence.

The general conclusion was of 'an underused penalty with considerable potential which had filled a key niche in the sentencing repertoire' or, as one senior probation officer put it 'part of the penal delicatessen .... as opposed to the staple fare of the criminal justice system'. But the biggest inhibitor seemed—still—to be the lack of clear guidance, the problems of inappropriate use and the desire of practitioners for more evidence of 'what works' when tagging offenders. It has been a recurring message, ever since the first pilot phase.

Meanwhile, despite good completion rates (over 80 per cent of offenders continue to complete their actual orders successfully) reconviction rates seem largely unaffected. The two-year follow up being undertaken from the second year of the trials shows 73 per cent of tagged offenders reconvicting within two years of sentence (Sugg, Moore and Howard, 2001), a result which, the researchers concluded 'although high, was no different to that of a comparison group comprising offenders who received other community penalties during the same period, and was also in line with predicted rates'.

EARLY RELEASE : HOME DETENTION CURFEWS

The slow—and, at times, excessively cautious—start to curfew orders as a sentence of the court gave no real indication of how a large scale tagging operation might work in Britain. Equally, cost analyses had assumed that tagging was comparable with other community sentences only by using a model that projected costs for 8,000 or 13,000 offenders. (Given those fairly substantial assumptions—they did not include start-up control centre costs, for instance—the Home Office gave the average cost at 1996/7 prices as: probation order £2,200, curfew order with electronic monitoring £1,900 and Community Service Order £1,700.) With the prison population continuing its remorseless rise this was soon to change.

The Crime and Disorder Act of 1998 introduced the home detention curfew (HDC) scheme as the first use of electronically monitored early release and it came into force at the end of January 1999. Under the scheme, most prisoners serving sentences of over three months and under four years would be eligible to be released on licence up to two months *before* their automatic release date, which was the half-way point of the sentence. (Thereafter, some would continue to be supervised on licence by the Probation Service, as before; others would be 'at risk' but unsupervised until the full expiry date of their sentence. Prisoners serving three months or under get remission only; those serving four years or more are eligible for consideration for parole. A complex system in which 'time served' already had little relation to 'time sentenced' was, in fact, going to become even more complicated.)

The point at which prisoners actually became eligible for release on HDC was graduated according to their sentence. The maximum time monitored was to be two months—it could be as little as two weeks. This was clearly going to be a 'no-risk' scheme from the political point of view, for experience with curfew orders suggested a 95 per cent successful completion rate should be achievable over such a short time scale. There were also some fixed categories who would not be eligible— juveniles under 18, prisoners required to register under the Sex Offenders Act, those with no fixed address, or awaiting deportation, and those who had earlier breached a curfew order.

The process of getting ready for the HDC was a chaotic one—new risk assessment systems and administrative checks in the prisons were needed, home visits to check suitability of premises (and the consent of others living there) had to be organized and the whole infrastructure of a truly national scheme set up, including control rooms and local staff recruited and trained. England and Wales were divided into four contract regions, three of which were awarded to the existing contractors for the curfew order pilot project. Securicor Custodial Services took the Northern part of England; Premier Monitoring Services (who now incorporated Geografix) had the London and Eastern, and Midlands and Wales regions. A newcomer, GSSC of Europe Ltd (a division of an American company already well established in electronic monitoring) took on the Southern Region.

But, a year after its introduction, it was clear that the scheme had bedded down with remarkably little fuss, although it had—again—been a cautious start. Home Office predictions were that 45,000 prisoners would be eligible for consideration in the first year and that the actual early release rate would be 50 per cent of this figure. In the event, prison governors, who make the individual release decisions, were much more reluctant to exercise their powers than had been forecast. Only 31 per cent were granted and the scheme has never, as yet, had to cope with the expected pressure of numbers. The reasons for this caution were not difficult to trace—the Probation Service had been told that there would be an assumption of release, but, just before the scheme started, prison governors were reminded that it was *their* decision and failure to exercise proper concern over risk was something for which they would be held accountable.

Already overburdened with a sea of new initiatives, performance targets, quality audits and inspections, and feeling that HDCs had been hastily introduced with insufficient attention to the messy business of actually making it work, governors decided to take no chances. 'They (politicians) invented it. But it's my head on the block,' one governor told me, when he received the Home Office instruction. 'If in doubt—don't let them out,' he added, ruefully. Most saw it as a failure of political nerve on the brink of new and uncharted territory. It is apparent, that, once established, this over-cautious approach will be difficult to shift without clear new Ministerial guidelines. Meanwhile, HDC contributes rather less than it should.

On its first anniversary, Home Secretary Jack Straw praised the 'remarkable success' of the scheme, claiming the expected 95 per cent success rate. Since his praise came at a time when the prison population had reached 68,000 and a further 4,000 rise was being predicted, however, his ringing endorsement might well have had other motives. Within weeks, publication of the first year results had divided politicians on predictable party lines. Conservative Shadow Home Secretary, Anne Widdecombe (whose party had, of course, introduced tagging in the first place) went on the attack, accusing the government of breaking its promise to be 'tough on crime' and to exclude serious and sexual offenders from the scheme. She produced figures showing that the first 18,000 prisoners released on HDC included those with the following offences:

Manslaughter	43
Attempted murder	5
Wounding	2,258
Drugs	2,207
Cruelty to children	21
Sex offences	18
Burglary	1,697
Robbery	717

and, since this was Britain, she added 18 offences of cruelty to animals (*Independent*, 29 March 2000).

The Home Office response, which did not challenge her figures, was to point out that all those released on HDC would have been out on standard release dates, within a few weeks, anyway. Ministers were not complacent about reoffending figures (quoted at 2.65 per cent by the

Offender Tag Association) but 'the overall compliance rate of 80 per cent compared favourably with other community sentences'. There was no attempt to explain the difference between Mr Straw's '95 per cent success' claim and this much lower figure.

Press comment was quick to seize on criticism of the scheme. 'Fifty tagged offenders go on the run' (*The Times*, 3 March 2000) was a typical headline and, unsurprisingly, anecdotal evidence tended to be wholly negative. Quite apart from the unfortunate incident in which a man had a tag fitted to his false leg, the story of the burglar who decided to go back to prison rather than continue living with his girlfriend (a decision which was presented as wholly unremarkable) was typical. What exercised the press was that, having unlawfully removed the tag, he reported to the nearest police station and was startled to be told to go home and await developments. He then waited 20 days to be re-arrested and returned to prison to complete his 14-month sentence (*Daily Telegraph*, 9 May 2000) .

In a large scale scheme, however, such opportunities for sniping were rare. Home Office research, as always, provides a comprehensive analysis of what has happened. A first year report (Dodgson and Mortimer, 2000) will be followed by more comprehensive analysis including the impact on prison and probation services, cost-benefit analysis, outcome measures and reconvictions. A presentation by the researchers at the Howard League Conference in September 2000 provided the following data:

- of 72,500 eligible prisoners, 21,500 were actually released on HDC (30 per cent);
- approximately 2,000 were on the scheme at any one time;
- so far 1,000 had been recalled to prison (5 per cent) although two-thirds of these had been for failure to comply with curfew conditions, rather than for a new offence;
- twenty-nine per cent of eligible male prisoners are released on HDC; for women it is 40 per cent and, generally speaking, the older the prisoner is (up to age 60) the more likely it is to be granted;
- the shorter the sentence, the less likely HDC is to be granted. This is largely because, with remand time, the process simply cannot be completed in time. Some challenge to this obvious unfairness seems inevitable;
- release rates are much higher for some offences (57 per cent for drug offences, 60 per cent for fraud and forgery) than for others (19 per cent for burglary, 22 per cent for theft and handling);
- there are also very variable release rates between individual prisons. Local prisons (24 per cent) might expect to be different from open prisons (73 per cent) but differences between similar-

type institutions cannot be explained in this way and there is much scope for improved consistency in the decision making process;

- release rates are similar between white and black offenders but Asian offenders are more likely to be released than either.

There is also a good deal of scope for improving the process, since there seems to be a real link between poor information provision and subsequent violations. Only 29 per cent of prisoners said they had been shown the explanatory video, for instance, and although 83 per cent said they had been given instructions and explanation in writing, it should have been 100 per cent.

Well over half of those interviewed self-reported a violation of the order at some point during the monitoring period, but only nine per cent had a formal warning—the others must have been of a minor nature, or undetected. The effect on the household was also the focus of attention:

- 22 per cent of curfewees said it had a positive effect;
- ten per cent of curfewees said it had a negative effect; and
- 12 per cent of curfewees reported problems arising between themselves and others in the home; over half of these related directly to the tag.

There were complaints that alterations to curfew hours (when the offender got a job, for instance) took too long to organize and more attention to the administration of the order is still needed. Finally, the researchers looked at the reasons that led to recalls. They concluded that most were due to:

- addictions;
- housing problems;
- lack of family support;
- institutionalised offenders who simply couldn't cope with a 'disciplined freedom';
- anger management; and
- 'hedonism'—a lifestyle that had more attractions than compliance with the order.

Reconviction figures are still being processed, but are being compared between a control group, HDC releases and those who applied but were not granted HDC. Preliminary results suggest that figures for this last group are high—but whether this suggests accurate risk assessments by prison and probation staff, or a group for whom short term monitoring might have a real impact, remains to be seen.

Tentative figures on the cost-benefit analysis of post-release tagging are so far giving a cost for the average 45-day curfew of £1,300. An 'uncrowded' prison place is costed at £2,150 per month so a year of the HDC scheme, saving 1,960 prison places, produces an estimated net benefit of approximately £37m. Preliminary reconviction figures (using six months after the normal discharge date as the cut-off point), and using a control group of similarly discharged prisoners taken from October/November 1988 who would have been eligible for HDC had it then been in force, show no real differences between the two groups. Of the HDC group 30.8 per cent reoffended; 30 per cent for the control group. Home detention curfews, it seems, are a good way of cutting costs with low-risk offenders by releasing prison beds; they have not yet met the stated aim of 'easing the transition' from custody to freedom, on which the government placed such emphasis.

Overall, HDCs have been a low-risk expansion of tagging—limited because of the cautious start, but well able to expand from what is now a secure base. Government enthusiasm has certainly not been in short supply—soon after the HDC results were made public the head of the Youth Justice Board, Lord Warner, was promising tagging as part of an intensive supervision package for the nation's 'worst' 3,500 teenage offenders and the Prime Minister was advancing it, on TV, as a method of dealing with domestic violence and stalking cases. The virtue of the HDC has been its role in establishing tagging as a credible option on a much larger scale than the curfew order had been able to achieve. It also made a national expansion commercially feasible, and therefore more cost effective. The message was clear—tagging was now an established part of the criminal justice armoury or, as Lord Warner spelt out in the House of Lords debate on the Criminal Justice and Court Services Bill (3 July 2000), 'We must face up to having a wider range of community punishments, properly enforced . . . using new technology to the maximum'.

ALTERNATIVE USES

One of the continuing problems of the criminal justice process over the last few years has been the collection of fines imposed on offenders. Despite the decline in the popularity of the fine, which at one time fell from use with a half of all offences to a third, and the aborted introduction of unit fines to link the penalty to the ability to pay, no real solution has been in sight. The Crime (Sentences) Act of 1997 was an attempt to strengthen fine collection by providing alternative penalties where there was reason to believe offenders would be unlikely to pay a fine. New measures were introduced on a pilot basis, including community service orders, curfew orders enforced by electronic monitoring and driving disqualification.

The two pilot areas were Norfolk and Greater Manchester. Community service orders (CSOs) were by far the most popular measure, accounting for 81 per cent of all orders in the pilot scheme in Norfolk, and 72 per cent in Greater Manchester. However 103 curfew orders, in total, were made on fine defaulters and, although detailed figures have not yet been released, an 82 per cent 'successful completion' rate is claimed.

The preliminary report on the scheme (Elliott *et al.*, 1999) reveals that the most common starting point was a series of motoring offences which had attracted the original fine. The offender could be released from the curfew order by payment of the outstanding fine, but most found it easier to complete the order than pay the fine. The average length of curfew was 50 days. There are some issues to be disentangled here, since the orders were only supposed to be made if the offender *would not* pay—not if they *could* not. It appears perceptions may differ.

The costs and benefits of the new system have yet to be assessed and the final report will compare the use of imprisonment for fine default before and after the pilots began.

At the same time as the use of curfew orders for fine default was being piloted, its use as a penalty for 'petty persistent offenders' was also being tested in the same pilot areas. A petty persistent offender is defined as a person who:

- already has one or more outstanding fines;
- has been convicted of another offence for which they *could* be fined; and
- would be unlikely to pay an appropriate fine for the current offence.

Here again, community service orders were also available as an alternative to a curfew order—and CSOs again proved much more popular (75 per cent of all orders). Seventy curfew orders were made, for an average of 70 days. Magistrates say they prefer community service because it is more positive and the offender is seen to be putting something back into society. They have continuing concerns about the powers available to deal with breaches of curfew orders and about how to decide the appropriate length of order.

More generally, there are some concerns that magistrates might begin to use the 'petty persistent offender measures' for other people, simply because they had lower than average means. To use it in this way, instead of a lower fine, might not be commensurate with the level of seriousness. This kind of 'ripple effect' on the decision making process, increasingly common as penalty options proliferate, does need to be kept in view. Britain already has a more comprehensive range of penalties available to courts than almost any other jurisdiction—whether it really needs to go on inventing still more seems doubtful.

The final report on these experimental additions to tagging use were not available at the time of writing, but it seems likely that they will be extended nationally, simply because the electronic monitoring infrastructure is available—and under-used. No such decision has apparently yet been reached on the third of the 'other uses' experiments: on bail.

Tagging as a condition of bail has been a longstanding option in the USA and, despite the failure of the earlier trial in England, it seemed an obvious choice for expansion. Existing curfews, which have to be enforced by the police, have fallen into disrepute since the police have no resources to monitor them, except in rare cases. But preliminary results (August 2000) showed slightly poorer results—42 of 196 defendants (21.4 per cent) were actually returned to court but almost two-thirds broke the curfew condition at some time in the order—even though it was allowed to continue.

> The study found that women played a crucial role in ensuring that their husbands, partners or sons obeyed the curfew. Women also experienced the downside of the system; the imposition of the curfews forcing men to remain at home between certain hours brought aggression and increased tension. A few families reported that the curfew led to an improvement in family relationships.
>
> (*The Times*, 10 August 2000)

What seems to be emerging in England and Wales, now that a comprehensive infrastructure is in place, is an 'all purpose' approach to tagging, with availability pre-court, as a sentence or part of a sentence and as a post-prison option; for juveniles (whom, with voice verification, we will consider later) as well as adults; and for just about every conceivable use from fine default to petty offences to domestic violence and a range of serious offences. Increased use certainly means more cost effective use of the infrastructure—but only if the new measures are cheaper or more effective than the ones they replaced. The Home Office, through the Research, Development and Statistics Directorate, is at least producing comprehensive data which will, within the next year or so, enable a judgement to be made.

Whether this scatter gun approach will be influenced by the data is something to which we will return. On 30 March 2001 the Home Office announced eight further 'principal fields' of electronic monitoring which were to be tested. They cover curfew requirements, exclusion orders and voice verification and will apply, among others, to dangerous offenders released under the new early warning scheme, tagging as a condition of parole; exclusion conditions as a requirement of other orders (probation, community service or licence) or as a separate exclusion order sentence. Most will be trialled from June 2001, and will continue to January 2004. The exception is the continuous tracking of offenders, which will be trialled later, 'when the technology has developed'.

What is absolutely clear is that with the infrastructure in place (and with both major schemes currently underused) the pressure is to expand and to make the most cost effective use of the contracts which exist. It makes economic sense. Whether it makes sense in criminal justice terms remains to be seen.

Note: Names of the principal community penalties in England and Wales were changed in April 2001. See p. vi for an explanation of these.

SCOTLAND

As so often happens, experience in Scotland provides a nice counterpoint to work south of the border. Electronic monitoring was introduced into the Scottish system in the context of Restriction of Liberty Orders (RLOs), which can require offenders to stay at a specified place for up to 12 hours per day, and for up to 12 months. The pilot project started in August 1998 and by September 2000 over 300 orders had been made. Media reaction was largely positive and a good deal of care was taken to design in effective liaison with the large number of agencies which would have an interest in their operation. National and local advisory groups were set up, the latter to cover the three Sheriff Courts in Aberdeen, Hamilton and Peterhead where the pilot scheme would run.

Evaluation was carried out independently, from the start of the scheme until March 2000, and the report from Lancaster University makes an interesting case study in itself (Lobley and Smith, 2000). A total of 152 RLOs were made during the first 14 months of the pilot, covering 142 individuals. The essential statistics were:

Age	16—20 yrs	54%
	21—25 yrs	26%
	over 25 yrs	20% (only 9 were female offenders)
Length	3 months	30%
	6 months	25% (75% were between 3-6 months)

More than two-thirds incorporated the maximum daily period of restriction, of 12 hours.

One notable feature was that 63 per cent of offenders made subject to RLOs had previously served a custodial sentence and a further eleven per cent had been remanded in custody. This compares with 54 per cent in the first phase of the English trials and tends to support the impression that targeting (in terms of replacing custody) was more closely realised in Scotland. The researchers suggested that RLOs replaced custody in about 40 per cent of cases, a crucial figure if cost effectiveness comparisons are to be made.

Of the 152 RLOs studied, 103 had been completed and nine were still in force at the end of February 2000. In the other 40 cases, orders had terminated as a result of the offender's failure to co-operate. The overall completion rate of 72 per cent, however, concealed a number of complexities, as the researchers were quick to point out: only eleven offenders completed their orders with no unauthorised absences and over half either had formal warnings or had reached the point where formal breach proceedings had been started (Lobley and Smith(1), 2000). Many orders had the tagging requirement suspended for weeks or even months due to remands in custody, or accommodation difficulties.

Some of the other results mirrored English experience—orders that ran concurrently with another community sentence were more likely to be successful than 'stand-alone' orders; longer orders were less likely to be completed successfully, as were those on younger offenders and those with more serious records.

So was it felt to be a successful pilot scheme? As always, there were fairly mixed messages. Certainly, the monitoring equipment worked well and there was only one case in which a tag was removed without detection. The views of sentencers, offenders, families and agencies were generally positive—although, as elsewhere, there was no clear consensus about who was most appropriate for an RLO. There were particular problems with young offenders whose heavy drug use and chaotic way of life made successful completion unlikely. This is in contrast with the early Norfolk experience, where tagging had a more positive role to play in bringing some structure into disordered lives. The time tagged may well be the crucial difference—compliance after three months does fall away markedly and there seems to be a compelling case for moving on to other programmes before this point is reached.

One of the disappointments in Scotland was that the contractors never had to work to full capacity, so not only was the system not fully tested—the cost effectiveness of tagging was never really demonstrated. In the interim report costs were actually given as if the usage had been based on full capacity monitoring and were £2,500 for a three-month RLO and £4,860 for a six-month RLO (Lobley and Smith (2), 2000). (This compares with £13,456 for a six-month prison sentence and £1,450 for a standard probation order.) Speculative savings were given if a national scheme were to be implemented, but before that happens, a consultation exercise is being mounted (Scottish Executive, October 2000). This is an unusually wide ranging review and the openness and clarity with which it has been mounted should make it a fascinating exercise. As the covering letter to consultees noted:

Electronic monitoring is still a developing technology which has considerable potential but is by no means a full solution to the range of challenges which our criminal justice system must face if it is to make our communities safer from offenders. We want to take a measured and considered approach to considering how far it can contribute to the wider criminal justice strategy; what the costs and benefits are; and the implications of its use for criminal justice agencies, for offenders or accused and for their families.

The press release added:

> Prison exists, and will always exist, for the most serious offenders. We don't believe that electronic monitoring holds all the answers—no single measure does. But it certainly can play a useful role in some situations.

The consultation paper sought views on various potential uses including bail schemes and the early release of prisoners; on assessment and suitability; on the duration and length of orders and on new technologies such as tracking.

To an outside observer, talking to a number of people involved in the Scottish pilot project, there has been some interesting learning. A number of orders had to be revoked because of a parent, partner or other householder withdrawing his or her consent to have the offender monitored at the given address. Despite prior agreement and careful explanation, the reality of living with the tag has produced pressures that no-one expected and it highlights the need to assess the wider impact as carefully as possible. One interesting example—which was successfully resolved with help from the contractor's staff—involved what seemed to be some very supportive parents who were fully agreed that their son, who was still living at the family home, should be electronically monitored. Family patterns were unusual in that the father worked away from home for two weeks at a time, then had two weeks off. The new complication was that his son, unable to go out during a 12-hour curfew, now had all his friends round to see him instead. The fairly delicate compromises to which the family had learned to adapt were suddenly fractured and the initial request was for the equipment to be removed, despite the potential consequences. In the event, some sensible family work was undertaken, new arrangements agreed and the order was completed successfully—but the domestic impact of longer orders is certainly one factor in deciding appropriate lengths.

As one participant noted, 12-month curfews are a very onerous restriction indeed—so the courts tend to set 'average' curfews much lower. If the maximum were to be reduced to six months, would the same process be repeated?

Breach proceedings in Scotland (where papers are returned directly to the Procurator Fiscal's office and action is not initiated by the contractor's 'responsible officer', as in England and Wales) have tended to be slower and, on occasion, rather less well presented because of lack of direct knowledge. There is a feeling that swifter, more certain breach action is needed before the scheme expands. The message will be quickly learned by offenders; it will also increase confidence from sentencers on whom, ultimately, so much depends. Anecdotal evidence suggests that breaches—and patterns of 'testing' behaviour—occur early on. Dealing with them, quickly and effectively, not only reduces the risk of further offending, but may encourage later compliance and a better outcome.

Whatever the outcome of the Scottish consultation, the relatively small scale and the care with which the design and preparation for the scheme have been undertaken make it a particularly useful model. A decision on future use will come in summer 2001; meanwhile the pilot courts are extending their use and by May 2001 had made 396 orders.

REFERENCES for *Chapter 2*

Dodgson K and Mortimer E, 'Home Detention Curfew: the First Year of Operation', *Home Office Research Findings*, No. 110, London, Home Office, 2000

Elliott R, Airs J and Webb S, 'Community Penalties for Fine Default and Persistent Petty Offending', *Home Office Research Findings*, No. 98, London, Home Office, 1999

Grant E, 'Electronic Monitoring Trial in Nottingham', *The Magistrate*, London, July 1989

Home Office (1), 'Curfew Orders Enforced by Electronic Monitoring', *Information for Sentencers*, London, Home Office, September 1999

Home Office (2), 'Probation Circular: Curfew Orders, the Role of the Probation Service', London, Home Office, 1999

Lobley D and Smith D(1), *Evaluation of Electronically Monitored Restriction of Liberty Orders*, Edinburgh, Scottish Executive Central Research Unit, 2000

Lobley D and Smith D (2), 'Restriction of Liberty Orders', *Research Findings*, No. 47, Edinburgh, Scottish Executive Central Research Unit, 2000

Mair G and Mortimer E, 'Curfew Orders with Electronic Monitoring—An Evaluation of the First Twelve Months', *Home Office Research Study*, No.1 63, London, Home Office, 1996

Mortimer E and May C, 'Electronic Monitoring in Practice: the Second Year of the Trials of Curfew Orders', *Home Office Research Study*, No. 177, London, Home Office, 1997

Mortimer E, Pereira E and Walter I, 'Making the Tag Fit: Further Analysis from the First Two Years of the Trials of Curfew Orders, *Home Office Research Findings*, No. 105, London, Home Office, 1999

Paskell CA, 'Supervising the Offender in the Community: Electronic Monitoring and the Spaces of Probation', MSc dissertation, Univ. of Bristol, September 1999

Scottish Executive, 'Tagging Offenders: the Role of Electronic Monitoring in the Scottish Criminal Justice System', Edinburgh, October 2000

Sugg D, Moore L, and Howard P, 'Electronic Monitoring and Offending Behaviour: Reconviction Results for the Second Year of the Trials', *Home Office Research Findings*, No. 141, London, Home Office, 2001

Walter I, Sugg D, and Moore L, 'A Year on the Tag—Criminal Justice and Electronic Monitoring Perspectives on Curfew Orders 12 Months after Roll-out', *Home Office Research Findings*, No. 140, London, Home Office, 2001

Whitfield D, 'Electronic Monitoring and the Probation Service Perspective', Speech to Home Office Conference, July 1999

CHAPTER 3

Current Use and Development: Europe

SWEDEN

As will be apparent from the brief history of tagging in the opening chapter, I regard the Swedish scheme as a model for any jurisdiction thinking of developing electronic monitoring. National and legal differences mean that 'carbon copy' schemes are unlikely, but the careful preparation, clarity of aims and very thorough way it was introduced and researched makes learning from the Swedish experience easy.

The scheme has had three distinct phases—a pilot project restricted to defined geographical areas during 1994-1996; an expanded (but still experimental) scheme for the whole country during 1996-1998 and, from 1999, a permanent sentence available as an alternative to short prison terms.

Ulf Jonsson, the Head of Department of client activities for the Swedish Prison and Probation Administration, described the background to the scheme in a paper to the first European Conference on Electronic Monitoring (Boelens *at el.*, 1998). In Sweden, he said, 25 years of trying various alternatives to prison had made little difference to prison use. Community alternatives were still seen as a soft option by sentencers and the public because they had very limited elements of surveillance and control. Electronic monitoring was designed to meet this criticism and offered real chances of improvement—but with the more complex selection needed, it also posed real dangers. Making sure everyone, from policy makers to front line probation officers, was clear about aims and objectives, was the first requirement.

The aims of the experimental scheme were listed as:

1. To provide more options;
2. To create a trustworthy and effective alternative to prison;
3. To reduce costs;
4. To reduce recidivism;
5. To reduce the prison population;
6 To test the viability of electronic monitoring; and
7. To develop new ways of working.

There was equal clarity in how the effects of electronic monitoring were to be measured, not just in the actual figures which would come from research, but in public satisfaction, the views of offenders, and its 'fit' in the overall range of penalties. It was acknowledged early on that electronic monitoring does not change behaviour, though it may have a useful stabilising effect. Longer term work would be needed for behavioural change and the title for the new order, 'Intensive Supervision with Electronic Monitoring (ISEM)', reflected the Swedish view that tagging could simply make a contribution towards the longer, more significant aim.

There was also an acknowledgement of the disadvantages of electronic monitoring—the intrusion into family life, the possibility of discrimination and the 'technical dependency' that such schemes create. This, he noted wryly, suddenly becomes compelling when the system crashes. The Swedes worked hard to maintain a balance between personal and technical supervision, and between help, treatment and control.

However careful the planning, good implementation holds the key to success or failure. In Sweden, the Probation Service was designated as the operator of the scheme, giving it responsibility for selection, 24-hour monitoring, follow-up of violations and the intensive supervision element—a comprehensive 'package' which is unusual, since there is more often a split between independent contractors and the statutory agency. Ulf Jonsson believed the critical success factors were:

- timing—'catching the mood of political and public opinion';
- support from top managers in the prison and probation administration;
- close working links between administrative and field staff;
- good information to external interests, including the media;
- adaptable staff, since new skills and training were needed;
- clear control measures and sanctions;
- good evaluation; and
- adequate resourcing.

As a comprehensive blueprint for a new scheme, it could hardly be improved.

So how does it work? An individual who has been sentenced to a short period of imprisonment (up to three months)does not, as noted earlier, proceed directly to jail. Sentences are served when prison beds become available (and, sometimes, to take account of individual circumstances) and this gap between the passing of the sentence and its execution is now used to ascertain whether ISEM can be used as an alternative.

The individual offender applies to the correctional authorities to serve his or her sentence on ISEM rather than in prison—the length of sentence remains the same. The ISEM 'package' involves the offender staying at home, except for time allowed and specified for employment, training, health care, participation in probation-run offending behaviour programmes, travel time, shopping for necessities and other similar tasks. The Probation Service usually allows for an hour out of doors on days when the offender has no other activities outside the home—this is a comprehensive and tightly regulated programme. Automatic electronic monitoring checks are supplemented by unannounced home visits, several times a week, and most of these involve a breath test to determine whether the person is complying with the ban on alcohol consumption. Drug use is similarly checked at the beginning of the supervision period and subsequently, when necessary. Add to this the weekly visit to the probation office for offending behaviour groups and checks at work (through a nominated 'contact person' retained by the Probation Service) and the message is clear—this may not be a prison sentence, but it will make real demands on the offender in return for his or her freedom.

All this is carefully explained at the start of the selection process. About 75 per cent of the target group go on to make a formal application for ISEM and, of these, 85 per cent are allowed to participate. (These and subsequent figures are taken from Somander, 1998 and Begler 1999.) The agreed plan must be the subject of written consent, not only from the offender, but from the people who live with him or her. This practical appreciation of the impact that monitoring can have on the whole family is typical of the care with which the programme has been devised.

Early views of the scheme were mixed. It came in for a good deal of criticism for being too easy a way to serve a sentence and too likely to be a soft option for people with money and a stable home. For others, it seemed the thin end of a mechanistic wedge which would replace human contact and proper efforts to rehabilitate. Staff worked hard to counter both of these. The requirement to pay (about £5 per day) for the use of the electronic monitoring equipment was waived for almost half of those involved, who had insufficient means, so that there was no discrimination on economic grounds; the intensive levels of contact and the compulsory groupwork emphasised that human contact and the need to deal constructively with offending behaviour were reinforced. Probation officers soon discovered that 'sensitive ears' and good listening skills were just as important in ISEM cases and that family issues often surfaced in ways that might, otherwise, have been less easy.

Criticism from abroad—especially Britain—centred on the people who were the subject of ISEM orders. Over half were drink drivers in the pilot project and, two years later, this was just under half and still the largest single group. But Swedish attitudes—and mandatory sentencing requirements—mean that drink driving really *is* a serious offence and will result in a prison sentence. Given the main aim of reducing the cost of imprisonment, it was an entirely logical target group. Other significant offence groups, all of whom had prison sentences of three months or less imposed, were assault (18 per cent), theft and property offences (nine per cent), public order offences (five per cent) and drugs charges (four per cent).

The results have certainly been impressive. Ninety-four per cent of those on the ISEM programme complete their order, with the remaining six per cent serving the balance of their sentence in prison. Fears that it would only be the lower end offenders (sentenced to one month) who joined the programme were unfounded—over 40 per cent of those eligible in the three-month, maximum, group were also selected for the scheme. Those on the programme spent an average of 30 hours a week at their usual place of work, so fears that it would simply be an expensive form of 'house arrest' were also groundless. Apart from electronic monitoring, home visits three times a week and regular drug and alcohol testing were also maintained, despite the growth of the scheme. Violations of the ban on drug or alcohol use were, in fact, the most common cause of failure and the trigger for a return to prison. These results have been achieved with large numbers, too. In 1997 some 3,800 offenders were on ISEM at some stage during the year, taking the number since the scheme started to almost 12,000.

Both offenders and families were overwhelmingly positive about ISEM and satisfied with the treatment they had received at the hands of the Probation Service. Although both acknowledged that some of the demands imposed by ISEM induced stress and threatened personal integrity, they did not do so to the extent that prison was seen as a better alternative. Attitudes had changed elsewhere, too. Kjell Carlsson, the project manager, said, 'Public, offenders,—even the media—think of it as a trustworthy, cost effective and credible alternative to imprisonment. And it has revitalised the Probation Service' (Boelens *et al.*, 1998, p.16).

Any community penalty which can claim such a result is worth examining in detail. Some of the acceptance of electronic monitoring in Sweden was a result of careful preparation and groundwork—no optimistic claims for what it might achieve, an extensive trial period with regular evaluation reports, and an emphasis on swift return to prison if the conditions were breached. But the additional requirement to pay for the use of the equipment was particularly shrewd, since the receipts went to a special reparation and compensation fund for victims. Even with only 53 per cent actually having the means to pay, over £100,000 had been raised in less than three years—a very tangible benefit.

The impact on the Probation Service was perhaps more surprising. The move to intensive 24-hour monitoring for a significant proportion of its caseload meant new skills, new staff and a very different approach to some of the work. Not everyone enjoyed the shift to more surveillance and control, even if it did come packaged with substantial rehabilitative measures as well. The probation officer who complained to me in the first year was by no means unusual, 'They're middle class, in good homes, fairly well off and well motivated . . . half of them shouldn't be on our books at all and the other half could do just as well on the intensive programme, without a tag'.

Gradually, as the offender base has widened and the possibilities of combining tagging with more traditional areas of work have become apparent, the mood has changed. Most staff realised only too well that a cautious start was a political necessity; most also realise that the Probation Service's willingness to undertake the new task has improved its credibility and standing considerably. This applies to other agencies as well as the wider public. Relationships with the police (who share the task of out-of-hours home visits, if necessary) are said to have progressed well. The message that the Probation Service is serious about preventing reoffending and will take prompt action if conditions are not kept has been a powerful one.

Sweden is the first European country to have published three-year reconviction figures for those tagged. This follow-up related to the 1994/5 cohort of the trial period—26 per cent had reoffended within three years, compared with 28 per cent of a corresponding group who served their sentences in prison. As the research report noted:

> A cautious interpretation might be that ISEM as an implementation procedure does not generally affect the convicted person's tendency to reoffend. At the same time, however, certain results indicate that ISEM may have a somewhat restraining effect on the tendency to relapse into drunken driving.
>
> (Begler, 1999, p.71)

Well before this research had been published, however, other results were very much to the fore—not just the successful completion rates, but the overall savings of money and prison places. One prison closed, another planned one was cancelled and within three years the prison population had been reduced by around 25 per cent. The Swedish system may be relatively small, in European terms, but these dramatic results do indicate what a well planned scheme can achieve.

Summing up the Swedish experience, the latest research report (Begler, 1999) is typically measured and restrained:

> As a corrective measure, ISEM is considerably cheaper than prison. The cost is ..... from 500-850 SKR less per day. Furthermore, ISEM yields substantial economic gains for society as well as for the individual since the convicted person can usually continue working at his ordinary place of work, thereby avoiding loss of income. It is clear that ISEM both eliminates the negative effects of prison and consumes fewer resources.
>
> ISEM seems to be at least as intrusive as prison when it comes to limiting the convicted person's freedom of movement during the time he or she is at home. However, the electronic technology employed in conjunction with ISEM cannot be used when (they) are outside the home. When he/she is at the workplace or elsewhere outside the home, the limitation on freedom

of movement is not as thorough as it is in prison, and neither is the Probation Service's ability to check up on the individual concerned or to institute measures in the event of rule violations.

A key question is whether the possibility of limiting the convicted person's freedom of movement as thoroughly as happens in prison is necessary for ISEM to be perceived as an entirely credible alternative to prison. This is not likely to be possible with the available technology at a reasonable level of personnel resources. The possibility exists, however, to develop ISEM in a direction that better corresponds to its prescribed goals by means of quantitative and qualitative increases in the level of supervision at the workplace.

The Swedish vision of the future, it seems, lies in improving the tried and tested (and relatively cheap) systems already in use, not being seduced by newer, more sophisticated and more expensive systems such as satellite tracking. The other planned development is to use electronic monitoring in a post-release scheme for prisoners serving sentences of two years and over. This is scheduled to start on 1 October 2001. Numbers will not be large—perhaps 400 a year, with a decrease of only 80 or so in the daily prison population. Meanwhile, and despite its success, numbers sentenced to ISEM are actually dropping and, by mid-2000, were around 30 per cent fewer than the previous year. The reason is that community service for offenders has been promoted and extended and courts (who do not have a say in the use of ISEM) have been keen to use it. The prison and probation administration see this as wholly positive—a wider choice should mean a more effective range of penalties if they are sensibly used and they have always been aware of the dangers of over-use if tagging was seen as a success. The Swedes remain, proportionately, the biggest users of tagging as a sentence, however, and what they have achieved is unique.

THE NETHERLANDS

Developments in The Netherlands provide a very useful alternative example of European practice and, together with Sweden, offer a ready made example to the many other countries who have visited to see a working scheme before starting their own pilot programmes. It was as long ago as 1988 that electronic monitoring was first considered and an advisory committee reporting to the Ministry of Justice looked at the options. The first real issue was whether it should be used at all—violation of privacy rights, in particular, exercised the national lawyers association, the academic community and the Association of Judges—and the general view seemed to be that it had little to offer.

Cost effectiveness was, in the end, the real spur. It was estimated that saving 350 prison cells by using electronic monitoring would save G20m per year—enough to overcome doubts and begin a pilot project. It was decided to trial it as both a 'front-door' (court sentence) and a 'back-door' (post-prison) scheme and the Probation Service was chosen to operate the scheme in partnership with a commercial contractor who would provide the equipment and the necessary installation, plus the 'out-of-hours' telephone service.

Han van der Leek, the Deputy Director General of the Netherlands Probation Service, explained some of the thinking behind these decisions:

> We are not against punishment. Abolitionism is nearly extinct in the Netherlands. What we are against is imprisonment that serves no other goal than to isolate the offender during a certain period of time. Because our European culture makes little use—or none at all—of actual lifelong imprisonment, we must always be aware of the offender's eventual return to the community. Plain imprisonment will then have no other than negative consequences.
>
> The Dutch Probation Service takes a constructive position within the penal chain .... so we participate actively in the execution of community sanctions, penitentiary programmes and electronic monitoring. Our strict condition, however, is that such sanctions are always combined with programmes oriented towards resocialisation. To give an example: the Probation Service is *not* available for the execution of electronic monitoring replacing preliminary custody for the sole purpose of saving cell space.
>
> (van der Leek, 1998)

It is therefore not surprising that, like the Swedes, the Dutch made sure that electronic monitoring sentences were always part of a treatment 'package'. The two target groups selected were:

- longer term prisoners who would be allowed to serve up to six months of their sentence under electronic monitoring—the actual time depending on the total length of the sentence; and

- offenders who would have received a prison sentence of up to a year, had electronic monitoring not been available.

Both were to be within the framework of existing legislative provision. By the end of 1998 about 350 cases had been started, with an average daily caseload of around 70 and the results had been sufficiently encouraging for a national scheme to be agreed, phased throughout 1999.

It was clear early on that the bulk of orders would come from the 'back-door' scheme and that the courts were much less sure of how it might fit in terms of the community-based sanctions they already had. Less than 20 per cent have come direct from courts. No category of offender or offence was excluded—instead, individual risk assessments were undertaken in what was a fairly cautious start. It was also very successful in achieving 90 per cent positive completions and (by

September 1999) only one reconviction for a further offence during monitoring from the first 500 participants.

Drug and alcohol testing is carried out only in those cases where it has been identified as a particular risk factor. The offence profile is very different to the other two major European schemes, because of the emphasis on post-release cases:

- 20 per cent drug offences;
- 19 per cent burglary;
- 12 per cent murder, manslaughter or attempts;
- 10 per cent robbery; and
- 10 per cent sexual offences/child abuse.

The average length of time tagged is three-and-a-half to four months. Offenders' partners or housemates are always asked for their agreement to the order, usually in a separate interview.

Right from the start it was made clear that electronic monitoring was not simply about a curfew—it was part of a 24-hour programme in which specified time is allocated to programme activities, 'socially accepted' activities, free time and time at home. Programme activities, which average 30 hours each week include work or work-training schemes, education and participation in probation-run treatment programmes. 'Socially acccepted' activities may cover anything from sports to church attendance—and are randomly monitored in order to make sure they are attended as agreed.

'Free time' is where the Dutch scheme differs from almost any other. Participants are told they have no general right to free time in the sense of being able to go or do what they wish, except for two hours on Saturdays and two hours on Sundays. After one month of successful monitoring this may be doubled, and doubled again after eight weeks. Only after three months can they earn a weekend off. Small scale breaches of conditions, like lateness for the start of a monitoring period can also result in the withdrawal of 'free' hours as well as an official warning. Against this highly structured programme, the 90 per cent successful completion represents a significant achievement. In the pilot phase, about 16 per cent of the successfully completed orders had an official warning, but monitoring was allowed to continue.

At the beginning of 1999 a new 'Penitentiary Law' was introduced. One important element of this was that prisoners who had served at least 50 per cent of their original sentence could (and other options were available) spend the last part of that sentence outside prison. A condition would be that at least 26 hours each week were part of a planned programme of activities and, for most, that electronic monitoring would also be an integral part. The test for using electronic monitoring would be whether it provided 'added value'. For instance, if a condition of early release specified attendance at a residential drug centre, then tagging would not be added on top of already considerable requirements.

Plans were made for 1,600-1,700 releases a year under this scheme, greatly extending the impact of electronic monitoring. In the event, they were less than half that and revised estimates for 2001 are down to an annual throughput of 800, saving approximately 200 prison places. Does this mean that tagging has failed to make an impact?

The Netherlands is fortunate in having one project manager only for electronic monitoring, right through from the preparatory stages. Ruud Boelens described, in a lively conference speech, what he thought lay behind this downward turn:

> The new penitentiary programme had no real implementation plan, like we developed for electronic monitoring. So there was confusion everywhere. Prison and probation staff are not sure what to do, so policy is actually made in the field, day by day.
>
> Prisons have also developed regimes over the last couple of years in which offenders have a great amount of freedom. In open prisons, offenders may be able to go home every weekend, and work outside the prison during the week. They may only see their cells on Monday to Thursday nights. So they see electronic monitoring as much more restrictive and they choose not to apply.
>
> (Boelens, 1999)

At the same time, prison pressures had decreased significantly—at one time there were 1,000 empty cells in the system. So the pressure to use electronic monitoring faded, too.

Ruud Boelens is philosophical about the relatively slow growth and says that it is fortunate that there is no great political pressure to do it faster. Better to have a cautious, well established scheme (and it has certainly attracted widespread media interest) than the policy lurches which are all too often the result of more hurried initiatives. He is also convinced that it has demonstrated that it is a useful tool:

> I believe in the usefulness of electronic monitoring. I have seen the contribution it can make to the reintegration of offenders. I also believe that we should be careful in the way that we use it. If we want it to be a real alternative to imprisonment, it has to have a rather tough character. At the same time, we as a Probation Service should use it as a means to contribute to change offender behaviour.
>
> (*ibid*)

Now, some of the structural difficulties have now been recognised and a new report *Sanctions in Perspective* has specified three kinds of penalties:

- fines;
- 'limited freedom' penalties. These include a range of community sanctions—probation, community service, electronic monitoring—graduated in seriousness and restrictions and aimed at dealing with a wider proportion of people outside prison; and
- prison—with fewer options for early release and with the last third of the sentence always on supervised licence.

Within this framework, the place of electronic monitoring seems secure. A pilot 'halfway house' scheme involving area monitoring is planned for 2001 and post-release electronic monitoring seems set to increase.

FRANCE

The French pilot project of electronic monitoring started on 20 September 2000. The Ministry of Justice had decided on four sites for a nine-month evaluation period and although the pilot scheme is very small—just 20 units at each of the four sites, with an intended throughput of 60 at each site during the pilot phase—there are ambitious plans for national expansion from the summer of 2001, in two phases of around 1,000 offenders each.

There are several distinctive features of the French scheme, the first of these being that it is entirely prison-based. Explaining this, the consultant who advised on the project said they had to decide:

> Who should be in charge of offenders that are under electronic monitoring—prison officers (guards) or probation people? This was regarded as a crucial decision, because it was going to reflect the whole philosophy of the system: is electronic monitoring an aid towards reintegration or is it an alternative to incarceration? The Department of Corrections decided that, although significant resources would be allocated to social work, electronic monitoring should primarily be regarded by offenders as a way to serve a sentence. Therefore, the persons who will monitor the offenders are going to be prison officers. Monitoring centres will be located on prison premises. In the same vein, offenders will get hooked up inside a prison, in a procedure similar to an incarceration procedure. The government wanted to maintain a strong psychological impact. It would not have been the case if the registration and 'tagging' procedure had taken place in the offender's home or in a judge's office.
>
> (Johnston, 2000)

The four regions involved are Marseilles, Lille, Bordeaux and Lyon. Marseilles and Lille seem to have been chosen because of particular prison overcrowding problems; Bordeaux because of its proximity to the French judicial college and Lyon because of the rural nature of the area covered. All the sites are located in low to medium security prisons.

The French say, modestly, that they have created nothing new; that elements of their programme can be found in both North America and elsewhere in Europe, both of which were trawled for ideas. But the French judicial system ensures a different emphasis. There are not only regular sentencing judges, but also a category of judges who follow up on the way sentences are served. They will provide first-hand information on the way sentences have been affected by electronic monitoring and their views are likely to be influential when decisions on the final shape of the scheme are made.

In the meantime, the range of experimentation is quite wide. Bordeaux is using the system for a conventional early release scheme; Marseilles as a 'work-release' type of sentence and Lyon for a probation-type sentence for offenders who had not previously experienced prison. Pre-trial use is not permitted under the current legislation and the view seems to be that a link to parole and early release is likely to be the foundation for any expansion nationally.

BELGIUM

A small scale pilot scheme started in April 1998 and continued until September 2000. At that stage new legislation became operational and electronic monitoring a permanent option, moving from its original base in Brussels to cover the whole of the country by the end of 2001.

The emphasis, right from the start, has been on early release from prison, with electronic monitoring as a condition of licence. It started by being available for prisoners serving up to 18 months, with up to three months as the monitoring period, but early growth was very limited because of stringent selection criteria and technical difficulties with both the systems being used—a conventional electronic monitoring system using ankle bracelets and a voice recognition system.

Selection was extended to sentences up to three years once the technical difficulties were resolved (the voice recognition project was abandoned) and the scheme now covers the last six months of the sentence. The aim is for up to 300 offenders to be monitored at any one time but those involved say this may take significantly longer than the original target date—perhaps two years or more. Sex offences against children, 'professional' trafficking in either drugs or humans and very violent offences are not considered compatible with electronic monitoring and the 'contra-indications' in the selection process (homelessness, severe drug or alcohol abuse, for instance) are the same as those used to assess for community penalties generally. Antwerp and Liege are next on stream and after a turbulent period in criminal justice generally, developments will be watched with interest.

SPAIN

Spain has announced plans for up to 3,000 prisoners to be curfewed at home as an alternative sentence and it was hoped that the scheme would start in the spring of 2001. At the time of writing it seemed doubtful if this target would be met, but the autonomous region of Catalunya has proceeded independently and began its own pilot programme on 20 December 2000. It is a small scale project, restricted to 25 cases (20 men and five women) in the first instance but the initial feedback has been very positive—the equipment performing well, offenders comfortable with the demands of the system and staff certainly keen to ensure its effectiveness.

ITALY

A pilot programme in Italy, which would centre on three very different areas in the north, centre and south of the country, has been under discussion for about two years now—but with interruptions, including a general election, very much part of the overall picture the delays are certainly understandable. To keep this in context, too, it is worth recording that the new legal framework in Italy was some 20 years in development, following the enactment of Law No. 354 in 1975. The reform gives effect to para. 27 of the Italian Constitution, which states that punishments must not consist of any treatment which is contrary to human dignity and that they must contribute to the rehabilitation of the offender.

Writing about the effect of the changes, one distinguished commentator noted that supervision of prison sentences, and a new law which allows significant numbers of offenders to submit an alternative plan to a prison sentence, within 30 days, were part of this. But she added, when discussing the monitoring of offenders' behaviour:

> The task of monitoring clashes with the concept of help and tends to mechanise the role of the social services .... There is a risk of reducing professional activity to mere verification. To carry out monitoring in a purely formal fashion, unrelated to the process of treatment, produces a response in the offender which comprises simple compliance to the requirements imposed and increases the chances of manipulating the worker.
>
> (Giuffrida, 2000)

Whether or not this will result in electronic monitoring only being available with a parallel treatment option—as in Sweden and the Netherlands—remains to be seen. For the moment, a pilot project was just getting under way as this book was being finalised. Five different regions, each with a different contractor, will have up to 70 electronic monitoring units available. Since each region will have the possibility of 'sub-trials' a good deal of diversity will result and at this stage the police will be the key agency. Though small, the project has been well-funded and seems to be a genuine attempt to explore the full potential of electronic monitoring. It will be watched closely and should provide interesting learning over the next year or so.

GERMANY

There seems to have been considerable interest, and much discussion, over the last three years without anything very tangible actually happening. This seems largely to be a result of the failure to get enabling Federal legislation passed. A new draft law on prisons would have allowed electronic monitoring to replace short prison sentences but it failed to make its passage through parliament: 'dammed by the right as being not tough enough and by the Greens as being an affront to human rights', I was told.

Hamburg and Baden-Wuerttemberg states had both hoped to establish local projects under the umbrella of Federal legislation, but have not now done so. The only state to go ahead with a scheme has been Hessen, which opted to make electronic monitoring an 'additional measure' to suspended sentences with probation. The move has been criticised as simply net widening but in fact numbers have been far too small to make any discernible impact, either way, on the state's 6,000 prison population. After one year, and the expenditure of some DM750,000, just 16 people had so far been subject to electronic monitoring.

SWITZERLAND

A well resourced pilot project started in October 1999, spread over six cantons (local government areas). By October 2000 234 orders had been made, all in conjunction with a treatment programme. The pilot project report was due to be completed by March 2001 and should make interesting reading, not only in terms of outcomes, but also in the range of offenders subject to electronic monitoring orders. Some national discussion will follow, but the indications are of a very successful pilot leading to an established scheme. So far, almost all have been court orders, rather than post-release cases and 82% have been successfully completed.

REFERENCES for *Chapter 3*

Begler A-M, 'Intensiv-Överakning Ned Elektronisk Kontroll', *BRA-Rapport*, No. 4. Stockholm,1999

Boelens R, 'Electronic Monitoring in the Netherlands', CCJS/ACOP Conference, 1999, published in *Criminal Justice Matters*, London, 2000

Boelens R, Jonsson U & Whitfield D, 'Electronic Monitoring in Europe', Netherlands, 'sHertegenbosch, *CEP*, 1998

Giuffrida MP, 'Reflections on Developments in Community Sanctions in Italy', *CEP Bulletin* No. 15, June 2000

Johnston W, 'More on the French Solution to Electronic Monitoring', *JOM*, Vol. 13, No. 4, Fall 2000

Somander L, 'The First Year of Nationwide Intensive Supervision with Electronic Monitoring', *Kriminalvården*, Norrkoping 1998

van der Leek H, 'Electronic Monitoring in Europe', Conference Speech, Amsterdam 1998

CHAPTER 4

Current Use and Development: North America

Any attempt to draw a reasonably comprehensive and accurate picture of the current state of electronic monitoring in the USA has to start by acknowledging what an extraordinarily diverse criminal justice mosaic has to be described. At the end of 1999 there were over 3.75 million adults on probation and almost a further 750,000 on parole. There were more than 450 separate state, county or court agencies involved; trying to make comparisons or, indeed, look for consistent trends is an almost impossible task. More than one million probationers and parolees are accounted for by two states only, Texas (556,410) and California (446,460) but numbers, practice, available sentences and just about everything else vary widely from tiny rural schemes to huge urban programmes. (All figures are taken from Department of Justice, July 2000 data.)

Within these numbers—and also outside them, where 'stand-down' or bail schemes are concerned—are a relatively small proportion of electronic monitoring schemes. Assessing exactly how many there are, and of what type, is a curiously frustrating process, since there is no standard reporting or recording mechanism and the annual survey undertaken by the *Journal of Offender Monitoring (JOM)* covers manufacturers, not the impossible task of keeping up with operational schemes. Best estimates are that by early 1998 there were 1,500 programmes involving up to 95,000 offenders and bailees (National Institute of Justice (NIJ), 1999) although it is never clear whether this represents the number of units leased or purchased, or the number of units actually in use. For various reasons, current figures are unlikely to be much different—perhaps 100,000, or around 1.7 per cent of the potential 'market'. (For this purpose I have defined the market as the sum of the prison and supervised populations—a very crude approach indeed, but with the sole virtue that it makes international comparisons more realistic and achievable.)

For most people involved in the USA this is a very disappointing figure, given that electronic monitoring has been available for 15 years, and that electronic monitoring products are widely regarded as reliable. *JOM* surveys found that most agencies believe the 1.5 per cent figure should be much higher and that somewhere between 5-20 per cent of the corrections population could be supervised in the community with electronic monitoring. Some of the reasons are historically based and were discussed in the brief history of tagging (see *Chapter 1*); others are also emerging and are usefully illustrated in looking at the way policy and practice are moving in two major state users—Florida and Texas.

FLORIDA

Florida has been at the forefront of electronic monitoring developments since the very beginning and is rightly proud of its record of innovation. On 31 March 2000 it had over 14,000 offenders on various forms of community supervision, 843 on 'ordinary' electronic monitoring (slightly down from a peak of 900) and 344 offenders subject to GPS tracking (ground position by satellite)—the latest form of electronic surveillance and control. Research between 1993-1998 had been favourable—a 24 per cent increase in positive outcomes over non-electronic monitoring cases was claimed and the basic electronic monitoring equipment was still highly regarded and used well for curfew checks.

But the debate had moved on to deal with higher-risk offenders. Who needed to be tracked and for how long? What results might be achieved with the much more sophisticated devices now available? There were three hurdles, in any case, to be overcome. The first was the cost, which was three times that of conventional monitoring; this resulted in an initial request for 1,500 GPS units being scaled down to 350. The second hurdle was that continuous monitoring required a 24-hour response and 'on-call' staff had to be found in each region. Thirdly, the huge quantity of data produced by 'real time' tracking produced significant advantages, for example being able to send a warning to an offender who might be approaching a prohibited zone, but also huge management problems in analysing and acting on the information produced.

Staff were nevertheless convinced that satellite tracking offered the most potential and the 350 systems purchased were designated for use with the 'worst of the worst' in risk terms—mostly high-risk sex offenders and people with a record of violence. Operators were delighted with the pin-point accuracy of available data; one pointed out to me that in Arizona it was now possible to hire golf carts using GPS technology which could tell you, within two yards, how many yards were left to the pin when you stopped to play your ball. She went on, 'If you know someone is watching you that accurately—your behaviour changes. Also, the system archives offenders' movements. If you determine an offence was committed at 3.00 p.m. at a specific location, you can very quickly tell where all your GPS offenders were at that time, even if the check is six months later. That's pretty powerful stuff, too'.

Average length of use in GPS cases was eight months at that time and although there were the expected problems with equipment, battery life and offender compliance, nobody doubted that these could be resolved. By 2001 Florida expected to have increased their available GPS systems to 470—but this was at the expense of the basic monitoring equipment, which would reduce in capacity to 650 units. In other words, overall capacity would remain virtually the same. It is this scenario which worries many manufacturers. Enhanced capability comes at a price but correctional budgets may not increase. Reordering priorities then becomes the only option.

Research is not yet available on reconviction or compliance with GPS requirements. We were quoted costs of $11 per day per offender for supervision costs, but this was just after the state had apparently spent $1.5m on 180 new units, and it did not include enhanced staffing costs at the agency. It may take some time for realistic costs to emerge. For the moment, however, there was no doubt that GPS was seen as a key piece of the future picture. 'If we could GPS track all serious offenders,' I was told, 'and could then overlap their movements with crime mapping techniques .... We could cut crime by 20 per cent'.

Asked to be more specific about this optimistic conclusion, it became apparent that perhaps 8,000 offenders would have to be involved (and, presumably, to co-operate). It would also need a low-cost, passive device which would only download movements once a day or the system would be completely unmanageable. Nor had staffing implications really been scrutinised, displacement effects considered or periods tracked been much taken onto account. But it would, equally, be wrong to scoff. Experience in Florida is real, learning is quickly absorbed and there is a willingness to push the boundaries to achieve the required ends. It may take years for the cheap, effective technology to arrive to fulfil the dream—but Florida was determined to be ready for it.

TEXAS

The view of the corrections future from Texas looked, at the same conference, rather different, with electronic monitoring taking a more peripheral role. There, 'Community Partnership Councils' had been set up in each town to assist the probation and parole services (which are separate in Texas) and a whole range of programmes had been developed which embraced everything from the emerging community corrections movement, to 'zero tolerance' programmes and very imaginative prevention initiatives.

The Parole Service provides a representative picture. In 1999 it dealt with over 30,000 releases—19,270 on mandatory supervised release (MSR) provisions and 11,925 on parole, where the average length of supervision is two-and-a-half years. Some of these, such as sex offenders, have mandatory contact requirements (between five and ten per month, depending on risk assessments); about 3,200 cases, or just under ten per cent are electronic monitored. Graduated requirements go up to what is known as SISP—the Super Intensive Supervision Programme, where 172 specialist officers look after a caseload of 1,464 offenders.

Monitoring is supplemented by daily activity scheduling, which has to be approved one week in advance by the supervising officer; by a minimum of seven face-to-face contacts a month; and by a range of specialist programmes in which offenders are required to participate. The most imaginative of these was FACES, the Family and Children Enhancement Service. This is designed to reduce the chances of parolees' children offending—a long term investment, which concentrated on non-offending issues such as parenting practice and parent-child relationships. During the pilot phase half the families will be those where the parent is still serving a sentence, half where he or she is already out on parole licence. You may not be able to change the world, I was told, but if you can make headway with repeat offending and 'learned offending' (within a family context) you will make a real difference. Confidence in the value of a variety of methods and approaches is high—three-year follow up research has shown recidivism rates among parolees to have fallen from 53 per cent in 1992 to 35 per cent in 1999.

The place of electronic monitoring is significant (hence the ten per cent figure among parolees) but limited—a surveillance device which helps reduce the level of post-release control on a gradual basis rather than the abrupt captivity–freedom divide which is seen as so much more difficult to manage. The Texas Parole Division's investment in GPS tracking technology has been very cautious—currently one contract for 25 units only. Staff say it is not just a question of unit costs ($13 per day per offender compared with $2.70 per day on 'basic' home monitoring) but the very labour intensive requirements of current system if it is to be managed properly. The size and weight of the equipment, even if attached to a belt on the offender, and the way both it and the batteries need to be looked after also indicates a high level of co-operation is required. 'If they're that compliant and agreeable, why do you need them to be continuously tracked?' I was asked. 'And if they're not, and you're so worried you have to know where they are at all times, why the hell aren't they still in prison?'

It was not, of course, a question I could answer, but any jurisdiction which is considering implementing GPS systems needs to consider it carefully. In the spring of 1998 about 40 offenders, nationwide, were subject to GPS tracking in the USA. By March 2000 the number had grown to 635, monitored from 68 sites, most of which had very small numbers in pilot schemes (Renzema, 2000).

The main categories of offender involved were:

- domestic violence offenders who are seen as a threat to one specific person;

- paedophiles and other sex offenders;
- pre-trial (bail) releases in particularly high profile cases;
- work-release inmates in the final stage of a prison sentence; and
- parolees with a history of violent crime.

All this was before BI, the biggest manufacturer, had produced a GPS system (it claims 70 per cent of the home monitoring market in the USA, and 80 per cent worldwide). Few doubt that the cautious growth so far will be maintained once the BI system is released early in 2001.

I saw a demonstration of the new system in the summer of 2000 and, if all it promises is deliverable, then it will be a very powerful tool indeed. The company say they have waited to produce GPS equipment because, until now, they could offer no more satisfactory a system than anyone else. They now claim to have resolved the two major issues which have hindered progress:

- *reliability*—we are promised enhanced tracking capability so that signals can be received much more consistently when the offender is in a car or a building. (Scepticism this side of the Atlantic centres on whether the more traditional European methods of house building will negate these claims);

- *information management*—GPS systems produce data overload simply because they monitor and record information continuously (every minute). Software which allows this to be scanned, stored and downloaded later—but still picks up on specific data only, is the answer. The system will, it is said, double check on restrictions, whether of curfew times or exclusion zones; it will use a 'group detector' if offenders get together and it will automatically alert the agency or supervisor by e-mail, pager, fax or cell phone of particular problems.

The system can be accessed remotely via a laptop computer; it can provide historical as well as current data and quick access screens can give supervising officers (or police, or whoever is authorised) full details of the offender, the order and a digital photo whenever needed. Each unit needs four hours' charge per day for 16 hours' use and it will download stored information while charging. It measures 6" x 4.6" x 2", is worn on a belt clip—and weighs just 1 lb.

The contrast between the upbeat presentation from BI and the comments from those operating current systems could not have been more marked. I was particularly struck by one well established company's manager who said, of their own, existing system:

> You have to be honest with offenders about the limitations of the equipment and say to them—don't put it in the boot of your car, or under the seat. Also,

since it may not be able to work in the 'belly' of a building, point out that you'll know where he went in, even if he leaves without it. It's like pretending there are no blind spots in the cellular phone system. They know it's not true.

Is this the future face of electronic monitoring in the USA? Or, indeed, worldwide? Cost considerations alone suggest that developments may be slow—few people thought that prison budgets would be cut sufficiently to pay for large scale GPS use and if money had to be found from community corrections budgets, then equally difficult decisions would be necessary to determine the ratio between quality (GPS systems) and quantity (basic electronic monitoring). Would it be politically acceptable to reduce overall numbers monitored sharply in order to concentrate on perceived high-risk cases?

Informal discussions suggest it may be—a feeling reinforced by a study of research reports lodged with National Criminal Justice Research Service (NCJRS) on a whole variety of electronic monitoring programmes. When I wrote my previous book *Tackling the Tag* I went through well over 100 of these and the tone was generally optimistic. Visiting again in August 2000 there were less than half that number and the conclusions were a good deal more questioning. One study on drink drivers (who have always been a significant proportion of electronic monitoring cases) looked at the results of an experiment in which different groups of offenders were jailed, were sentenced to house arrest with electronic monitoring or were placed on an eight-week programme with treatment and counselling components. The differences in outcome were marginal; electronic monitoring, it was said, was simply cheaper and did not unduly jeopardise community safety (NCJRS, 1997).

A five-year study in Indiana detailed 22 per cent failure rates on electronic monitoring for adult offenders (regardless of whether they were first-time or repeat offenders) and 63 per cent failures in repeat juvenile offender cases. Others produced better figures—although often on small schemes—but the overriding impression was of increased realism of what might be achieved by the use of electronic monitoring. There are no lack of applications—Los Angeles county, for instance, uses electronic monitoring as a component part of the following programmes:

- intensive probation supervision;
- supervised early release;
- Work Furlough Home Detention;
- Juvenile Community Detention;
- gang members involved in drug related violence;
- Drug Offender Probation Orders;
- Home Detention Orders;

(Smylka and Selke, 1995)

What has changed is the emphasis on trying to determine how best it can be applied, including the most cost effective uses.

When I asked a group of manufacturers and service providers why the market seemed so static, they came up with three answers. First, that a competitive market has become a short sighted market. They have been so busy vying for existing business and cutting each other's throats that insufficient effort had gone into developing additional markets. Second, that poor targeting remained a problem and that electronic monitoring, overall, still suffered from poorly used schemes which, inevitably, produced disappointing results. Third, that development had been unnecessarily hampered by the complete lack of standardisation in the USA which meant that every state 'did their own thing'. Equipment testing (a requirement for approved tendering procedures) varied from state to state and had to be undergone separately (a costly process) for every state in which the manufacturer wished to tender. No one would accept other people's test results, least of all those in the UK which were much more rigorous but which a number of manufacturers had successfully passed.

The same manufacturers had their own vision of how electronic monitoring should develop. A secure and growing market, they said, needed much more agreement about how technology could be used to provide a graduated response to offending. Basic monitoring, voice verification and satellite tracking all had a part to play as long as they were recognised as complementary and not in competition. They form a valuable buffer between the 'all or nothing' sentences of prison or probation and they provide a response to the problems associated with both—the negative effects and costs of custody and the perceived need to exercise more control over offenders who are being supervised in the community.

Yet development has largely been generated by institutional overcrowding, not by programmes designed to meet specific needs. The lack of any national organization on the use of electronic monitoring and of any wide ranging attempt to determine electronic monitoring programme success has left it poorly placed to occupy specific parts of the overall sentencing continuum. Pleading for a more disciplined approach in electronic monitoring data collection, screening and selection processes the *Journal of Offender Monitoring* noted:

> The consequence (of current practice) is generally a mediocre program that is inconsistent in its delivery of services. Observation and field experience clearly reveal that many end-users fail to create a policy and procedure manual; many agencies have no explicit screening/selection criteria; some do not define electronic monitoring violations and possible sanctions; and almost no agency evaluates its program to determine the degree to which the program meets explicit goals and objectives. When we finally establish an electronic monitoring association, develop acceptable standards of

practice, create a national data bank on electronic monitoring and develop consensual screening and selection processes, we will be well on our way to systematising electronic monitoring programs that will enhance the likelihood of crashing through the 'electronic ceiling'.

(Cohn, 1999)

CANADA

The Canadian experience of electronic monitoring has attracted relatively little attention, over the years. This is partly because of the sheer size and diversity of developments in the USA and partly because, for long periods, nothing much seemed to be happening. There are, however, some interesting features which deserve a closer look and some recent research which, at least, asks some uncomfortable questions.

Canada—or, at least, British Columbia, for each province runs its own Ministry of Correctional Services—was an early user of electronic monitoring. A pilot programme started in Vancouver in 1987. It ran for a year, by which time 92 offenders had completed the programme and plans were then made to expand throughout the province on a phased basis. It was subsequently tried in all regions but was discontinued in the sparsely populated north-west of the province, where low numbers made it uneconomic. By 1996 it was averaging around 300 offenders on electronic monitoring and with costs estimated at less than half those of the 'open custody centres' it was replacing, it was judged to be successful, with recognisable benefits to the offender as well as economic gains.

Two years after British Columbia started its scheme, Ontario also experimented with electronic monitoring but with rather different results. A decision to abandon the scheme was taken because it was not judged to be cost effective and, ten years later, use is limited to monitoring 'temporary absence offenders' from prison, with a caseload of around 60. There has, however, been a policy re-think, helped by encouragement from the Ontario Supreme Court and by autumn 2000 there were plans to expand the scheme significantly, to consider its use with high-risk offenders and to examine other technologies such as voice verification and global positioning systems.

The other provinces to use electronic monitoring were Saskatchewan (from 1990) and Newfoundland (from 1994). Neither is particularly large, numerically but, with British Columbia, they illustrate the differences which make country-wide comparisons so difficult.

- *British Columbia*
  Post-prison scheme supervised by prison officers assigned to work in the community:
      time-tagged— seven days to four months (average 37 days);

successful completion—89 per cent;
recidivism after one year: 30 per cent.

- *Saskatchewan*

  Court-based scheme supervised by probation officers:
  time tagged— average 139 days;
  successful completion—86 per cent;
  recidivism after one year—17 per cent.

- *Newfoundland*

  Prison-based early release scheme combined with structured intensive treatment programme, supervised by probation officers:
  time tagged—average 72 days;
  successful completion—87 per cent;
  recidivism after one year—32 per cent.

Newfoundland targeted 'moderate-risk' offenders (low-risk offenders could be released without electronic monitoring) and the mandatory treatment programme, of nine hours per week, concentrated on substance abuse and anger management. Individual counselling and employment help were also available but the programme struggled to find sufficient numbers.

Saskatchewan, where the electronic monitoring order comes as part of a sentence of probation, had an average daily 'tagged' population of around 90. The province has the highest incarceration rate of aboriginal offenders in the country and the programme was specifically designed to operate as an alternative to prison for this group. Electronic monitoring participants of aboriginal origin tended to have higher-risk scores than non-aboriginals so this aim, at least, appeared to be being met. With 65 per cent of the province's prison population of aboriginal origin, there was clearly scope for action.

British Columbia's use needs to be seen in the context of an unusually determined effort to control the costs of the criminal justice system and to use community based options whenever possible. Deputy Minister, Jim Graham, spelt this out:

Although British Columbia's population has nearly doubled and its crime rates have increased, the population of British Columbia's adult correctional centres is the same as it was 30 years ago. For every offender in jail, there are ten under some form of community supervision. We like to think that we have given the citizens of British Columbia a good bang for their correctional dollar.

(Schulz, 1995)

The British Columbia scheme has no requirements in relation to treatment attendance; selection criteria are (a) minimum risk to the community (b) non-violent and (c) no more than four months of the prison sentence remaining.

After almost a decade of experience, the Solicitor General's office in Canada decided to evaluate the three main provincial electronic monitoring programmes in an attempt to answer the question: does electronic monitoring reduce the criminal behaviour of offenders? The results of that study (Bonta *et al.*, 1999) are instructive—and so is the use to which they have been put.

This was a careful piece of research, which collected detailed criminal history and personal-demographic information on 262 offenders under electronic monitoring supervision. These individuals were compared to 240 inmates and 30 probationers, matched on important offender and risk factors. The criminal activity of all the offenders was recorded one year after completion of their programme, or release from prison.

Despite the differences between the three programmes, the results were described as 'remarkably consistent':

> Being placed on an electronic monitoring programme had no appreciable impact on the future criminal behaviour of the offenders. They continued to engage in as much crime as those who remained imprisoned or those who received a sentence of probation. In addition, a significant proportion of the electronic monitoring offenders were sufficiently low risk to suggest that they could be safely managed in the community without the enhanced restrictions imposed by electronic monitoring.

Worse was to follow.

> Although a cost effectiveness analysis was not conducted, the findings cast doubt on the potential savings promised by electronic monitoring. The costs of purchasing equipment and monitoring low-risk offenders when alternatives such as temporary absences are readily available appear counter-productive. Supplementary analysis also showed that a reduction in criminal behaviour resulted *only* when some of the offenders were given high quality (offending behaviour) treatment programming.

The report concluded with three policy implications:

1. As long as electronic monitoring programmes target relatively low-risk offenders, and many of them do, they are unlikely to offer a cost effective alternative to imprisonment. Unless we can demonstrate benefits with moderate-risk offenders, electronic monitoring programmes may actually increase correctional costs by 'widening the net' without improving public safety.

2. In terms of long term public safety, the probability that offenders will re-offend after completing electronic monitoring supervision remains the same as for those who are not electronically monitored.

3. Correctional interventions that aim to reduce criminal behaviour are more likely to come from the application of treatment programmes rather than intensive monitoring programmes.

(Bonta *et al.*, 1999)

The message was as bleak and uncompromising as the overview research from the National Institute of Justice in Washington some five years earlier. So what was its impact on policy?

Ontario
Ontario provides the most interesting case study in trying to answer this question. The Minister of Correctional Services in the province had announced in October 1995 that he would introduce an electronic monitoring programme for adult offenders—and that he would finance this by closing 25 'halfway houses' which currently provided some 400 bed spaces. These were generally occupied by offenders who were in the community on temporary absence (work release) schemes and it was felt that anyone suitable for this level of freedom could probably be supervised effectively, and more cheaply, without the provision of housing.

The decision was a controversial one and pressure was brought to bear (not least by the agencies that provided the halfway houses) to have it reviewed. The result was a series of hearings before the Standing Committee on the Administration of Justice of the Legislative Assembly of Ontario, which took place in 1996. Among those called to give evidence was the American Probation and Parole Association (APPA). It is a strong supporter of electronic monitoring, although its position statement (APPA, 1998) prioritises good targeting, strictly defined performance standards and proper resources for enforcement.

Their evidence, however, was properly cautious. Warning the Committee about risks in connection with what were, generally, low-risk offenders already working in the community, its spokesman said

Research .... shows that you get the opposite effect if you provide intensive services to lower-risk populations, that is, you actually increase the risk of reoffending. With regard to electronic monitoring, earlier research results were unclear about the effectiveness of electronic home confinement in reducing reoffending. Most of the studies suggested that offenders on electronic home confinement fared no worse than those serving other community sanctions.

Reoffending rates *were* improved when electronic monitoring was combined with other programme interventions, for example drug treatment for substance abuse offenders. There is evidence that electronic monitoring became more effective when combined with other rehabilitative programmes.

Most jurisdictions look to electronic monitoring as a means to reduce costs and, if used appropriately, it can be cost effective. However, using electronic monitoring on low-risk offenders who could do as well on parole or other release programmes undermines its ability to save money and leads to over-provision of services, thus increasing costs. Also, as I noted earlier, providing intensive services such as electronic monitoring to low-risk offenders has been found to increase recidivism rates, further increasing costs.

Electronic monitoring is cost effective when used on moderate and high-risk offenders and coupled with appropriate correctional interventions that target specific criminogenic factors.

(Evans, 1996)

It was a remarkably clear message that Ontario, which had already started its new electronic monitoring programme, had got its targeting wrong. The Committee decided that Ontario's programme should therefore be evaluated with two issues in mind—cost effectiveness, and net widening as a result of the use of electronic monitoring as 'an enhancement to the remaining community supervision mechanisms instead of an alternative to such mechanisms'. In fact, numbers were still very small when the Solicitor General's research was published, primarily due to restrictive eligibility criteria.

However …. in autumn 2000 Ontario was set to expand electronic monitoring significantly. I asked why, given the province's own previous experience, and the disappointing research results, they were prepared to try again. The answers, from several sources, were consistent and could just as easily have come from civil servants in England, policy makers in the USA or politicians in half a dozen European countries:

Because the public can see we are doing something about reducing risk. Tagging is a very obvious way of reassuring them.

Because we're tough on crime—that's the message. It's all much more punishment oriented and the public want their pound of flesh. We can do it through tagging much more effectively than by increasing prison use.

But could they sell it to the public as cost effective, and justified by results?

Well … we are going to move towards using it with more high-risk offenders—that would be in line with the research. But I guess we'll be pretty cautious for a while, yet. If you think this is more style than substance …. well, the government can choose to spend its money any way it wants, I guess. Dealing with crime is mostly about perception, and people's fears. Things like sex offender registers, which we are also introducing, and tagging, have an impact on people's perception of what politicians are achieving. I guess that is the most important thing of all.

As has often happened, the short term gain in introducing electronic monitoring has been achieved by politicians. Working through this to achieve effective schemes that make a real contribution to criminal justice policy and practice is a longer and more complex process.

REFERENCES for *Chapter 4*

American Probation and Parole Association, *Position Statement on Electronic Monitoring*, Lexington, KY, September 1998

Bonta J, Capretta SW and Rooney J, *Electronic Monitoring in Canada*, Ottawa, Solicitor General's Office, May 1999

Cohn A, 'What We Know About Electronic Monitoring', *JOM*, Vol . 12, No. 2, Spring 1999

Dept. of Justice, *US Correctional Population, July 2000-10-26*, Washington DC, Bureau of Justice Statistics 202/307-0784,

Evans D, 'Electronic Monitoring—Testimony to Ontario's Standing Committee', *Perspective'*, Lexington KY, Fall 1996

National Institute of Justice, 'Keeping Track of Electronic Monitoring', *National Law Enforcement and Corrections Technology Centre Bulletin*, Rockville MD, 1999

National Criminal Justice Research Service, 'Effects of House Arrest with Electronic Monitoring on DUI Offenders', Research paper 168209, National Criminal Justice Research Service, Rockville MD, 1997

Renzema M, 'Tracking GPS—a Third Look', *JOM*, Spring 2000

Schulz D (Ed.), *Electronic Monitoring and Corrections*, Vancouver, Simon Frazer University Press, 1995

Smylka J, and Selke W (Eds.), *Intermediate Sanctions: Sentencing in the 1990s*, National Criminal Justice Research Service, 1995

CHAPTER 5

Other Jurisdictions

Although the largest developments involving electronic monitoring have been concentrated in North America and Europe, they are by no means the only ones and a brief review of experience elsewhere—and expected developments—is a useful way of completing the current picture.

SINGAPORE

Singapore was early in the field with electronic monitoring used as part of a home release programme. This forms part of a much more comprehensive treatment and rehabilitation regime for drug addicts. In describing 'Operation Ferret', which launched it in 1977, the then Commissioner of Police was quoted as saying 'we have compulsory treatment and rehabilitation for every drug addict we ferret out'.

The treatment period may be for up to three years and starts with a residential rehabilitation centre for all those who have been medically examined and certified as a drug addict, or who have themselves volunteered for treatment. The five-stage residential programme is followed by up to two years of community supervision, with regular urine tests, group counselling and other aftercare services—and up to six months on electronic monitoring. Numbers grew steadily, reaching a total of almost 3,000 in 1993. The programme was an ambitious one and electronic monitoring was certainly seen to be part of its success. Forty of the staff involved were themselves tagged for between two and four weeks before the system became operational—perhaps the best way of understanding both the strengths and weaknesses of the system. The programme is still in use, although current caseload numbers have proved more elusive to track down. After a three-month leisurely exchange of e-mails, mostly designed to elicit why I wanted the information and what I was going to do with it, and despite the fact that similar information had already been given to me in relation to the prison scheme, the correspondence came to an abrupt end in April 2001 with a message reading, 'I regret to inform you that we are unable to furnish you with the statistical information you require. Thank you for your interest in our organization and warm regards'. It ended with a quote from Mahatma Ghandi: 'Strength does not come from physical capacity. It comes from indomitable will.' Faced with such a will, I retired, baffled. It remains an interesting example of specific use within a well targeted programme.

In May 2000, electronic monitoring began a second sphere of use in Singapore, as a post-prison, early release scheme. Prisoners eligible must be non-drug, less serious offenders and I was told that, in the first six months, most were 'white collar' offenders, who were seen to pose little risk while the scheme became established. Depending on the length of sentence, prisoners can be released up to six months early, with eligibility starting once the halfway point of the sentence is reached. Typically, a prisoner serving a six-month sentence, would be released one month early, on electronic monitoring. Some 200 prisoners have benefited so far—the average daily caseload in January 2001 was about 60 and officials were confident that a measured expansion would be possible. They certainly see electronic monitoring as an established part of the criminal justice process there.

AUSTRALIA

Electronic monitoring was first used in Australia in 1988 with a small scale scheme in the Northern Territories aimed at establishing home detention in remote Aboriginal communities and reservations. It was followed in 1989 and in 1991 in South and Western Australia respectively, with New South Wales starting its own scheme some five years later. Given the range of developments and the time they have been established, it is interesting to note how slow subsequent growth has been. As one manufacturer pointed out to me, it had been the land of promise for so long that most of those original promises were now being made again.

New South Wales has emerged as the largest user, with up to 400 units available (although never at full capacity) over its two schemes. The first of these is a 'front end' sentencing option, with the electronically monitored home detention order (HDO) set as a genuine alternative to prison. Sentencers have to set the term of the prison sentence, in open court, before then deciding if they will refer for HDO assessment. If suitable, the time served on the HDO is served 'day for day'; if not, the prison sentence has to be imposed. The scheme operates from the seven major urban areas and Ken Studerus, its Director, is clear that electronic monitoring is a tool to make Home Detention work, not an end in itself. 'We're pretty staff intensive—caseloads of ten or twelve per officer— because these are probation and parole programmes, primarily'.

The other 'alternative to custody' element comes when offenders breach orders on New South Wales' periodic (weekend) detention order scheme. The Parole Board, which oversees this, now has the power to revoke a Periodic Detention Order (PDO) and refer for Home Detention assessment, rather than simply ensure the balance of the term was simply served in prison. This is an important new power, since fairly high breach rates have always been associated with PDOs. They make up a significant proportion of the offenders on the Home Detention scheme which currently has a total caseload of about 170.

Of those who come straight from court, I was told most can be classed as 'repetitive low-risk' offenders (where risk of reconviction may be high, but seriousness is not the main issue) or as serious welfare fraud offenders. This offence has traditionally been seen as meriting custody, often for significant terms and, given the 'day for day' rule on electronic monitoring periods it has led to offenders being monitored for up to 18 months. Successful completion rates are good—though this is, of course, an a-typical group.

The second part of the New South Wales scheme is in monitoring temporary release from prison—either day release, which is normally for work or educational reasons, or for weekend release towards the end of a sentence. Checking is done by officers using 'drive-by' units, which means that there is no intrusion at the workplace, and travel arrangements can be unobtrusively checked, too. Around 100 prisoners are released in this way at any one time and it is felt that electronic monitoring has enabled temporary release to be expanded with some confidence.

But growth, overall, has still seemed much slower than expected. As a sentence of the court, it was felt that quite specific 'hurdles' had to be in place to avoid net-widening. But that, in turn, has left sentencers much less willing to use it. Originally it was felt that a post-release 'back door' scheme would provide major growth in electronic monitoring and, indeed, a workable scheme was in the planning stages. Unfortunately, the minister in charge was not only arrested on corruption charges, but ended by serving his sentence in one of 'his' institutions. Politically, I was told, it is off the agenda for some years yet ....

Elsewhere in Australia, growth of any kind has been slow indeed. South Australia had 165 offenders on electronically monitored Home Detention early in 2001; Western Australia had 63 plus another 25 on monitored bail. The Northern Territories, which still has a Home Detention scheme, no longer uses electronic monitoring.

In two states with no existing usage, moves are also under way—if cautiously. Queensland has long had Home Detention arrangements, together with other community release programmes. But it has checked these by telephone and face-to-face contacts. Now a pilot programme is starting to see if the schemes can be widened for those deemed too risky for release under the lower levels of contact. Numbers are likely to be small. Finally, Victoria is taking an active look at both court and prison based schemes. I was told that they were late in the field for two reasons—first, a well organized and strong civil liberties lobby, who have consistently opposed electronic monitoring and second, because their proportionate use of prison is low, leaving the case for electronic monitoring rather less easy to establish.

NEW ZEALAND

Legislation in New Zealand authorised the use of electronic monitoring as far back as the Criminal Justice Act of 1993, but it was two years later before a Home Detention pilot programme started. It was a small scale, carefully monitored scheme and the results were not entirely encouraging (Church and Dunstan, 1997).

Thirty-seven offenders were monitored following early release from prison. One was actually returned to the prison for non-compliance during the pilot programme—eleven more reoffended with two years of completing it. Also, because probation officers were expected only to supervise between seven and 12 offenders at any one time, costs were disproportionately high, comparable to prison.

However, a permanent scheme started in October 1999—again, a 'back door' early release scheme for prisoners serving not more than two-year sentences. It is the sentencing judge who determines whether any offender serving more than the normal two-year maximum should be able to make an application for consideration and cases of serious violence are precluded. Maximum eligibility is one-third of sentence.

The variety of schemes in Australia and New Zealand should enable some useful comparisons to be made, once sufficient experience has been gained.

SOUTH AFRICA

Reference has already been made to the ambitious plans in South Africa to introduce what would become the largest single scheme in the world, in order to reduce chronic prison overcrowding. In mid-2000 the proposals, which were proceeding towards formal tendering, had created a considerable stir in the world of electronic monitoring, not least among service providers, who were exploring local partnerships with equipment suppliers as well as assessing the particular difficulties which difficult terrain and a less developed infrastructure would bring.

And then it all went horribly wrong with corruption scandals surfacing—and implicating senior figures—and an abrupt halt to plans which were already far advanced. But the problems—endemic overcrowding, especially among the increasing pre-trial population—were already reckoned to be almost unmanageable and electronic monitoring had been accepted as part of a three-part crisis strategy:

quick fixes—immediate short term gains: actions and procedures across departmental boundaries which could be implemented quickly, and with:

- fast track projects—solutions which could deliver results within about 18 months. Electronic monitoring was the most important of these;
- enterprise level projects—major projects which would affect all core processes in the criminal justice system. Six were identified, including one which would establish a technology infrastructure for the justice system.

(Fanaroff, 2000)

Electronic monitoring is thus seen as a temporary expedient and whether it becomes a more permanent feature of the criminal justice landscape will, I was told, depend on the experience which will be rapidly gained. But the scheme still stalled at the tender stage (in May 2001) and the frantic efforts to get it back on track so that a start can be made in five separate regions have yet to bear fruit. South Africa's starting point has so many obvious parallels with the USA that it will be interesting to see what has been learned, what pitfalls avoided. But there are huge differences, too—of equipment, of software in particular. While the scale might not be as great as the 30,000 early released prisoners (over three years) envisaged at the start of the scheme, it will be watched and analysed closely as electronic monitoring's next big step.

REFERENCES for *Chapter 5*

Church A and Dunstan S, *The Evaluation of the Home Detention Pilot Programme 1995-97*, Wellington, NZ Ministry of Justice, 1997

Fanaroff B, 'The Integrated Justice System', *Nexus* (South African Correctional Services Magazine), April 2000, Pretoria

CHAPTER 6

Making it Work

Getting the technology right and making sure that its use is targeted to the most appropriate offenders are the two main requirements of a successful and effective electronic monitoring scheme. But there is also a third component—making it work—which needs equal attention if the scheme is to be sustained. Partly, of course, this is about operating standards, whether by public or private bodies, and work is beginning with CEP to see whether agreed best practice standards can be developed in Europe.

But it is much more than that. 'Making it work' covers a whole range of issues including co-operation between the different agencies involved, dealing with the impact on families, defining which technologies will work for which offenders and responding to violations. This chapter brings together a range of issues which come under this general heading.

TECHNOLOGY PROBLEMS

Despite huge advances over the last ten years, it would be foolish to pretend that electronic monitoring technology is now foolproof. Anti-tamper security devices have certainly made removing the tag illegally almost impossible—but the word 'almost' still needs to be retained. Just one person in the Scottish pilot project was able to 'slip' the tag and go missing, but the fact that one person had been able to do so had a disproportionate impact. It is also difficult, sometimes, to establish exactly what has happened—manufacturers and service providers have a vested interest in keeping any breaches of security quiet.

The case, early on, in the English pilot project which made national headlines when an offender 'went missing' was a reminder of how much confidence can be shaken. Sorting out the reality of what happened from the urban myths which gain instant currency can also be a problem. Just before curfew orders with electronic monitoring were made available nationally in England and Wales, an enjoyable story was doing the rounds about a young offender, newly tagged, who kept his leg in the freezer for half an hour, at home, so that his ankle shrunk sufficiently (with the help of liberal quantities of Vaseline) for him to slip the tag off—and place it on his mother's ankle instead. She then kept scrupulously to the curfew conditions while he continued with his normal patterns—and this went on for a month until an unscheduled home visit by the monitoring company revealed the truth. Despite extensive checks, I have never been able to confirm this story, but it still surfaces from time to time.

Literature in the USA still accepts that there *are* ways of removing most—if not all—anklet transmitters in such a manner that tampering is not automatically detected (Conway, 1998). Proper inspection procedures should establish when this has happened and it is generally accepted that it occurs in only a tiny minority of cases. But no statistics exist on the incidence of this or any other technical problems and, at present, no one sees it as in their interest to collect or publicise such figures.

Other technical problems do surface from time to time. There was some surprise in August 1999 when the Prisons and Probation Minister for England and Wales accepted publicly that the rapid expansion of tagging into the new Home Detention Curfew scheme had revealed a range of problems. The report went on to say:

> a design flaw means they (tags) do not work if prisoners live in high rise blocks or have big metal objects such as iron baths or kitchen ranges in their homes .... Signals are blocked by the metal objects or by high altitude(!), setting off false alarms in the security base station. As a result, about 20 prisoners have been wrongly sent back to prison'.
>
> (*Independent*, 30 August 1999)

In confirming the report, the Minister said also that tagged offenders who live in large buildings are being asked to restrict their movements to certain rooms so that the tag signal is not lost.

Since then, further work—and experience in setting boundaries and being aware of potential hazards—has improved the situation. But it reinforces the message that electronic monitoring is by no means suitable for all offenders at all locations and that alternative options need to be considered when accurate, reliable signals are not obtainable. One alternative, voice verification, will be discussed later in this chapter. In the meantime, checking on these 'false alarms' needs to be particularly carefully undertaken. Such cases are, however, a tiny minority of the total electronic monitoring caseload. It is just that errors—or room for doubt—are especially undesirable when someone's liberty may be at stake.

The fact that boundaries can be determined according to individual circumstances makes the initial home visit, in which the equipment is fixed and the boundaries set, a crucial one. The general rule of thumb seems to be that boundaries are set as closely as possible to include the back and front doors to the property, but absolute accuracy to a defined boundary is simply not possible—although offenders are never told that. There is, in any case, a good argument for adopting a fairly flexible approach to boundary setting. In some jurisdictions the back yard or garden is included so that family ball games can be permitted when a parent is tagged; one of the first women prisoners in England to be tagged made it clear that having the boundary round her block of flats set sufficiently widely to enable her to take her dog out at night made all the difference (Hart and Mistry, 1999).

Most offenders invest the system with rather more capability than it actually has. This is partly due to its being new, partly because it *is* sophisticated electronic equipment and we are all used to being amazed at advances in technology. Experience in the USA suggests that, once the system becomes more familiar, offenders will use considerable ingenuity in trying to circumvent it. But for most of those whose periods tagged are short, I wonder how much it is really worth it? The context here is somewhat different to the much longer periods that were often used in the USA—and where house arrest or home confinement often meant very little freedom at all. In England and Wales, with a maximum tagged period of 12 hours each day there is nothing like the same level of restriction.

What is clear is how much depends on the quality of field staff who undertake the installation of monitoring equipment. The two-week training course operated by Premier Monitoring Services covers installation and calibration, equipment checks and tampers, induction procedures, cable laying and remote antennae and fault finding procedures in exhaustive detail—but most staff accept that until you go out and 'do it for real' the learning has only just begun.

Once technical details and installation have been resolved the emphasis shifts to the day-to-day management of cases and the recording of incidents and their response. The way a control room operates is described in more detail in *Chapter 8* but the essentials are:

- a swift response to any alarm or incident which suggests conditions are being violated. (Much of this is 'testing' behaviour and occurs early on. A correct, timely response much improves the chance of longer term co-operation.) An immediate telephone call to the offender to check on the position is the best starting point. A home visit from a field officer can be used later, or in serious cases where a formal warning seems likely;

- a clear policy and an efficient response to requests for changes in the curfew hours. This is one area which has been the subject of many complaints in England and Wales. Variations may be needed for many legitimate reasons—a change of job, child-care arrangements, public transport difficulties—but the separation of powers between contractor, court and probation service makes for cumbersome arrangements which often create, rather than resolve, difficulties;

- control room staff who can spot 'trends' in offenders' behaviour which might be the precursor of further trouble. A gradual pattern of being just a few minutes late, or out of range for very short periods .... might well enable an alert operator to resolve a minor problem before it became a major one.

After two years of curfew orders on a national basis most problems leading to violations were fairly predictable:

- 54 per cent had missed a whole curfew period;
- eight per cent had removed their personal identification device (PID); and
- 18 per cent had recorded cumulative absences over the allowed limit of two hours per calendar month.

It is, therefore, very much a minority who require the attention to detail that is suggested above. But that 20 per cent who don't come into a clear-cut breach situation do need skilled and confident handling from high quality staff.

FAMILY ISSUES

From the very beginning, it has been recognised that home curfews affect not only the offender, but also those with whom they live. As we have seen elsewhere, a significant aspect of the assessment and selection process is the likely family impact and most good practice guidelines include a requirement to consult partners or other family members before orders are made. However careful the explanations, however, it is not possible to capture the extent or the reality of the day-to-day intrusion which electronic monitoring inevitably brings.

Particular caution has always been used in cases where domestic violence had been recorded or suspected; or where there were child protection issues. Enforced proximity resulted in some tragic cases of domestic violence in the early days of tagging—and some understandable caution thereafter. It is, however, an under-researched area, although published work tends to be fairly reassuring. Canadian studies (Doherty, 1995; Mainprize, 1995) claimed that around half of all respondents said monitoring had 'no effect' on household relations and one in five said positive benefits accrued—from 'bringing us closer' to improvements linked to other programme requirements such as abstinence from alcohol. And a resounding 78 per cent said, 'no' when asked, 'Has your home become like a jail'? There are, of course, families driven to distraction by the enforced presence of one member and no one should underestimate the pressures this sometimes imposes, for *all* family members then feel they are sharing in the punishment. But there are many others where it is clear there are real gains for individual offenders:

Half the offenders reported home detention caused big changes in their lives. Work and family related changes were most often cited. Many offenders indicated they were absent from work less often than had been the case before home detention. Indeed, many offenders worked overtime or took a second job in order to be out of the house for longer periods of time .... For a good number of individuals, the *structure* imposed by house detention, however monitored, produced desirable results. They had a chance to 'dry out' and review their life; got to know their family again and worked more often while they were being monitored.

(Baumer and Mendelsohn, 1990)

Rather less positive views came from both offenders and their families in the study by the Home Office of home detention curfews in England and Wales. Although 97 per cent of curfewees were, not surprisingly, in favour of the scheme which had allowed them early release, only 22 per cent said the period of monitoring had had a positive effect. Ten per cent said it had been negative; 12 per cent reported specific problems between themselves and another member of the household, over half of which were directly related to the tag. Families, asked separately, produced very similar figures (Dodgson *et al.*, 2001).

The fact that there are no easy answers to the likely impact of electronic monitoring in family terms is well illustrated by the variety of comments recorded in the Scottish Restriction of Liberty Orders evaluation (Lobley and Smith, 2000). Some parents spoke of the onerous sense of responsibility they felt, 'going out looking' for their son when a curfew period was approaching; another remarked that 'we are now unpaid warders'. One mother, who thought her son had done better on the order than she could have imagined, said she agreed to it without really giving it much thought, or knowing what it might entail. She thought, 'Oh dear, what have I let myself in for? .... But in fact it all went fairly well with no real problems'. Her view was influenced by the simple fact that she thought it would avoid her son returning to prison, since last time he had come out with a worse drug problem than when he went in.

There seems to be a widespread view among sentencers and report writers that electronic monitoring is likely to be unsuitable where domestic violence is a cause for concern, there are child protection issues or other family issues relating to carers, mothers and pregnant women. Physical or mental health problems are also seen as an 'unsuitability' indicator. But these are a minority of cases. What is needed in the majority is a clear and realistic explanation to family members about the impact of monitoring on the household, and on relationships, when initial assessments are made—and an offer to discuss any tensions or pressures later, once the order is in force.

This is relatively easy to achieve when electronic monitoring is combined with another community penalty, or with a supervised period of licence. It is almost impossible if tagging is on a 'stand-alone' basis. Operational staff have shown during pilot projects (when both numbers and pressures are low) how valuable such interventions can be. Few believe it can ever be sustained in the large schemes now operating. But if the figures produced for the Home Detention Curfew scheme are a guide, such help could make a significant contribution to success rates—and, ultimately, to reoffending.

CO-OPERATION BETWEEN AGENCIES

The structure of electronic monitoring schemes varies widely, but most involve some kind of partnership arrangements. Within Europe, for instance the following variations are all in place:

- the private sector supplies equipment, but the probation service operates the programme, runs the 24-hour control centre and deals with all violations and day- to-day issues (Sweden);
- the private sector supplies equipment and runs the 'out of hours' scheme and all other requirements (Netherlands);
- the prison service runs the scheme but operational oversight is assumed by a judge (France);
- the private sector operates the scheme, the control centre and all action on violations; and day-to-day contact with offenders. The Probation Service undertakes assessments and may supervise in tandem, under the terms of a community penalty (England and Wales); and
- as England and Wales, but the prosecution of violations (i.e. once information is laid) rests with the courts (Scotland).

Given that there is a significant 'third party' which is responsible *either* for the making of the court order *or* for the release on licence (in which case it is the prison governor rather than a magistrate or judge), it will be apparent that good communication and clarity of roles are essential. Nowhere is this more evident than when the curfew order may come as part of an overall package—as it usually does—where different agencies may be responsible for different aspects. Sweden solved this by making the probation service responsible for the whole order and ensuring that electronic monitoring was an integral part of the intensive supervision scheme. In England and Wales, where the separation between electronic monitoring (carried out by the contractors) and offending behaviour work (the responsibility of the Probation Service) is absolute, there is real scope for confusion.

For the most part, however, the results seem to be good. After a period of understandable caution and some suspicion field staff from both agencies do cross check when circumstances seem to warrant it; do talk to each other when difficulties arise and do share views when breaches mean a fresh report to court and the possibility of resentencing occurs. More often, the two sides of supervision are acknowledged, but deliberately kept at arm's length. There is something about the impersonal authority of the tag which makes it easier for offenders to accept; something about the discipline it imposes which means the probation officer can develop the longer term 'treatment' objectives without some of the authority battles which so often characterise the start of supervision.

There is a long way to go before anyone can claim to have the balance exactly right and for the moment contractors' staff throughout the UK say their main concern is the *lack* of help available to offenders on 'stand-alone' orders. Pressure of work (as well as the tightly drawn contracts within which they operate) means that little more than routine checking and following up of violations is possible. Yet front line staff say how aware they are of the basic help (with employment, benefits, drugs and alcohol) that many offenders on 'stand-alone' orders still seem to need. 'It's not advanced social work,' one field officer told me, 'it's pretty basic stuff. But it needs time to sort through issues even if you're going to refer them on—to an alcohol agency, for instance. And time is the thing we haven't got'.

The early research on the pilot projects in England and Wales produced figures suggesting that, far from doing worse (as might be expected with no extra help) 'stand-alone' orders actually had a slightly higher successful completion rate than those made in conjunction with other community penalties, such as probation. But these figures are misleading, as the researchers accepted. First, the 'stand-alone' orders were generally on less serious offences and less heavily convicted offenders and so would be expected to produce better figures. Second— and only time will tell how significant a factor this is—the results covered a period when low numbers and the restricted coverage of the pilot projects meant that staff *could* give extra time and attention to those on 'stand-alone' orders. There were extremely positive examples of this in both Manchester and Norfolk in the early years; staff in both areas have subsequently expressed real frustration that this kind of 'added value' work, which is in everyone's interest, is no longer possible.

NEW POSSIBILITIES

As the technology develops—and so sentencers and report writers become more confident in using it—the range of cases which may be appropriate will also expand. This poses real questions of training for both groups—good targeting is already an issue, without the complexity of added options. Two examples currently head the list of new possibilities: exclusion orders, which may use tagging to prohibit an offender from entering a specified place; and voice verification, which demands a separate section on its own.

Exclusion orders

Exclusion orders were made possible by sections 36B and 40A of the Powers of Criminal Courts (Sentencing) Act 2000. (They were already available, but not used, in the Scottish Restriction of Liberty Orders experiment.) Section 62 of the Criminal Justice and Court Services Act 2000 made similar provisions in respect of prisoners released on licence with an exclusion condition. The maximum length of an exclusion order is two years—and there is no specified maximum where it is a condition of licence.

The primary aim is, of course, the protection of victims. Parole licences often contain 'no contact' provisions of this kind, but there is no way of monitoring them properly and their impact is limited. The new orders aim to make full use of what is known as 'reverse tagging'. Early interest in reverse tagging in the USA was centred on domestic violence cases, where, either in conjunction with a restraining order or after one had been broken, courts would order the offender to be tagged, wearing the PID transmitter in the usual way. The Home Monitoring Unit (HMU), however, was placed in the home of the person (usually the estranged wife) who needed some protection. Only when the transmitter came within range of the HMU (and this was usually about 70 yards) was the control room alerted and the police despatched. The problem, of course, was the very limited protection that such a short range actually provided—it may have made detection more certain but there was no possibility of preventing any violence, if that was the aim of the offender in breaking the order. Most schemes were discontinued because of this.

Domestic violence cases are not, however, the only group for which a more robust reverse tagging scheme might be helpful. In the autumn of 2000 I was approached by the Network for Surviving Stalking, whose founder, an enormously courageous young woman named Tracey Morgan, wanted the new anti-harassment legislation (largely based on her experiences) to be backed up by technology which would offer more practical, as well as legal, protection. She was working with the Central St Martins College in London whose 'Design against Crime' scheme was already established.

Contact with manufacturers established that a 400 yard 'safety zone' (more in particularly favourable circumstances) was now technically possible and this, together with the new legislation, may at last give some victims a measure of both protection and peace of mind. The offender would not only wear a PID, as normal, but have an HMU in his or her own home, so that any curfew requirements could be monitored; the person needing protection would also have the HMU installed (and this could be at home, at work, or both) and the 400 yard 'exclusion zone' would offer a real measure of protection *and* a way of proving a breach of any court order, which is currently a major stumbling block.

In case this seems an over-reaction, it was not until I met victims of persistent obsessive stalking and heard the harrowing details of what they had undergone that I had any idea of the true scale and seriousness of the issue. Victims may be pursued for years, with an intensity that defies belief and the sheer, accumulated pressure of never knowing if your pursuer is round the next corner, watching your house or ready to confront you becomes unbearable. The 1998 *British Crime Survey* recorded that most stalking lasted for no more than three months—but that one in five victims was stalked for more than a year. And for some, it goes on for four or five years. The full extent of the problem was confirmed by a study *The Nature and Extent of Stalking* (Home Office, 2000) which suggested that half a million victims are subject to violence or threatened with attack each year.

Moves are now under way to mount a pilot project from the summer of 2001 in three separate areas, using the existing electronic monitoring network and contractors. If successful, it could make a real contribution to the needs of victims—admittedly a relatively small number—in some very worrying cases. More generally, if tagging can be perceived to be making this much more positive contribution, its role in the criminal justice system is likely to be more securely established.

Voice verification
The same legislation—the Powers of Criminal Courts (Sentencing) Act 2000—which enabled pilot projects on reverse tagging to start, also (section 36B) provides for national trials of voice verification schemes. This is based on the same principle as the electronic monitoring of curfew orders in that it checks whether someone is at a specified place at an agreed time. It differs from electronic monitoring in several respects:

- it is intermittent rather than continuous;
- no device is worn by the offender, and there is no special unit to be installed at the offender's home;
- it is infinitely flexible—monitoring can be at any location with a land-line telephone; and
- it is much cheaper.

Provision is also being made (section 62 Criminal Justice and Court Services Act 2000) to test it with prisoners released on licence.

I first became interested in the potential for voice verification systems in 1996, when I saw the Voice Track system in use in the USA. At that stage it was being used exclusively as a money saving device—a cheap way of retaining contact with and checking the location of many low risk probation cases where high caseloads meant that personal contact was impossible. It seemed to me, however, that there was real potential to use it—not in competition with tagging—but as an adjunct to supervision, for improving offender accountability in high-risk cases and with a wide range of supervision options.

The system works by registering an initial voice sample when an order is made—a simple process that takes less than five minutes and can be accomplished from any digital telephone, perhaps in the court house. That 'voiceprint'—said to be as unique as a fingerprint—is then stored and is checked every time a subsequent call is made. This allows two checks within a few seconds—that the right person is calling; and that the location (through the 1471 system which reveals the caller's number) has been agreed as part of the schedule set for the offender. That schedule can be set daily, if required, and can cover a range of agreed locations—the offender's home and place of work, a drugs clinic or treatment centre, for instance—so that a simple home curfew check can be easily extended. Calls can be made at prearranged times to ensure the offender keeps to the schedule; alternatively he or she can be issued with a pager so that random checks can be made. The pager simply alerts the offender to register with the call centre within an agreed time, usually a few minutes, and the check against agreed locations is automatic, with the supervising officer alerted (also by pager) if violations occur.

Printouts on offender compliance can be made available on any given level, depending on the perceived risks in individual cases. Thus, the immediate warning by pager would only be used in very high-risk cases; a daily or weekly printout might well be sufficient, depending on the nature of the case.

The Kent pilot project

I wanted to see whether the system would work as well on the UK telephone system and whether we could demonstrate its reliability and accuracy in the way I had seen it operate. We also wanted to gain a clearer understanding of who might be most usefully supervised on this kind of process. The Home Office provided the money for a pilot project in the Kent Probation area and a Project Manager, Joan Farrall (to whom I am indebted for much of the following information), was appointed.

The equipment was delivered and installed in May 1998 and testing and technical checks took another five months before we could start accepting referrals in earnest. Members of staff went 'live' on the system to start with and did their best to test it out by using wrong locations, wrong PIN numbers, missed calls and even close relatives with (it was thought) identical voices to try and subvert the system. All were duly rejected and although, under field conditions, speech from the offender can be corrupted by extraneous noises, in general the system worked exceptionally well. If there are problems, and the new voiceprint does not match sufficiently well, the offender can be asked to repeat the process a few minutes later, or the supervisor can be notified.

Six months later, 25 cases had been, or still were, being supervised using Voice Track; 14 on probation orders, including four difficult and risky sex offenders, eight on community service orders and the other three in bail or prison release cases where additional controls were felt to be needed for public protection reasons. None of the offenders committed new offences, although two cases were terminated because of offender violations and one finished early when it was decided that the risks were so great that continuous police surveillance was a safer option.

The following case example gives some idea of how Voice Track was used.

Christopher L was a sex offender against children for whom a tight schedule was organized. During term time he was tracked every half- hour from 8.00 a.m. to 10.00 a.m., and again in the afternoon between 3.00 p.m. and 6.00 p.m., which kept him in the house while schoolchildren were going to and from school. On Saturdays and Sundays he had more flexibility in his schedule.

When Mr L was first on Voice Track he complied with his ring-in times extremely well. During the second week he had a few instances of 'failed voice'. We could hear things were not going well with him by his voice patterns, which changed on a regular basis although not so much that his voice could not be positively identified. He was also becoming quite angry and ringing the Voice Track manager regularly. On one occasion he failed a contact from his designated number, and the programme manager dialled the number which came up on her pager immediately. The number was a public telephone box situated in a local town some way from Mr L's home. At 12.00 a.m. he phoned in on schedule from the right location and was contacted at home to ask where he was for his 10.00 a.m. call-in. His false answer was challenged immediately. The incident—and our immediate response—had a significant effect and Mr L completed the Voice Track period successfully.

Other cases included two volatile, risky young men in a probation hostel, for whom it was felt that the simple night time curfew was insufficient and, at the other end of the scale, offenders on remote community service placements for whom Voice Track checks were a useful cost saving device. In removing the need for physical checks, much time and money was saved and it was the potential the technology has for most cost effective supervision in rural areas that led the Home

Office to expand the pilot project to cover the North Wales probation area.

The pilot programme finished with 74 orders successfully completed, just over half of them the 'low-risk' cases where cheap, simple checks can save huge amounts of supervisor time. Thirteen cases were on juvenile offenders and the Youth Justice Board for England and Wales was sufficiently impressed to start its own voice verification project for young offenders, which the adult scheme will now replicate.

As new options become feasible, the pressure on sentencers and youth justice and probation workers to be well informed about appropriate and effective use will increase—and amid the welter of new initiatives constantly being heaped on overworked criminal justice agencies, this will be no easy task. 'Making it work' has a long way to go and is going to need good quality advice from central government as well as adequate training for front line staff and decision makers. Technology does what it is asked to do very effectively—offenders rather less so. Using one to help the other still requires good research, sensitive use, consistent operation and a real understanding of how best to reduce reoffending—none of them easy in the clamour for instant results.

REFERENCES for *Chapter 6*

Baumer T and Mendelsohn R, *The Electronic Monitoring of Non-Violent Convicted Felons: an Experiment in Home Detention*, Indiana University, 1990

Conway P, 'Technology—it's Time for the Truth', *Journal of Electronic Monitoring*, Vol. 11, No. 3, Summer 1998

Dodgson K *et al.*, *Electronic Monitoring of Released Prisoners: An Evaluation of the Home Detention Curfew Scheme*, Home Office Research Study 222, London, March 2001

Doherty D, 'Impressions of the Impact of the Electronic Monitoring Program on the Family', *Electronic Monitoring and Corrections*, Schultz K (Ed.), British Columbia, Simon Fraser University, 1995

Hart S and Mistry U, 'I Love my Electronic Ball and Chain', *The Big Issue*, No. 325, London, March 1999

Home Office, 'The Nature and Extent of Stalking', *Home Office Research Study*, London, October 2000

Lobley D and Smith D, *Evaluation of Electronically Monitored Restriction of Liberty Orders*, Edinburgh, Scottish Executive Central Research Unit, 2000

Mainprize S, 'Social Psychological and Familial Impacts of Home Confinement and Electronic Monitoring', *Electronic Monitoring and Corrections*, Schultz K, (Ed.), British Columbia, Simon Fraser University, 1995

CHAPTER 7

Impact on Policy and Sentencing

The growth of electronic monitoring in criminal justice systems has rarely seemed to be part of a carefully targeted and coherent policy towards the sentencing of offenders and overall crime reduction. This is particularly true of England and Wales, where the approach was more on the lines of, 'Well, it's available so we'll see what it might do' and, more explicitly, where it was provided on an un-targeted basis so that it might 'find its own level'. The willingness to experiment on this basis has gone well beyond the initial curfew order pilot scheme and the subsequent large scale expansion to prison early release schemes; it has embraced its use for fine defaulters, petty persistent offenders, juveniles and bailees. There are very few offenders who come outside the potential market for tagging.

Opinions vary as to whether this is an open minded and refreshingly unblinkered approach which can be modified as soon as research results enable options to be clearly chosen; or a quick fix for politicians who want short term solutions because of the difficulties of addressing serious crime reduction agendas, and for whom it has become an easy replacement for a more coherent approach. Tagging remains one of the most visible and easily understood sentencing options—and, therefore, one of the easiest to present in policy terms. The continuum stretches between those who regard it as a new toy—'the magic bracelet'—and those who see technology as the only sure way of enforcing community sentences and, therefore, as an indispensable aid.

Any attempt to measure the impact on policy and sentencing has to consider rather more than statistics. It needs to include the overall policy climate, other parallel changes like the community justice movement and the remorseless 'talking-up' of prison which has long outlasted Michael Howard's strident claim that 'prison works!' It needs also to try and identify the specific contribution that tagging can or does make.

What is it that, uniquely, tagging offers in an already bewildering range of sentencing options? The obvious claim is that it tackles parts of offending behaviour that other sentences cannot reach by providing surveillance and control; by daily and physical reminders of the sentence of the court and the implications of non-compliance; and by imposing a disciplined framework which will enable other options such as probation intervention to be developed without undue risk.

It also does so at a fraction of the cost of what is perceived as the main alternative—time in prison. In 1999 the average annual cost of a prison place was £22,649 and, although Category C and open prisons were below that figure (at £17,543 and £14,405 respectively) and might be considered as the places where costs were most likely to be saved, the amounts are so much in excess of the £1,800 quoted for a curfew order that the case seems overwhelming.

And yet .... those savings are only real if we can be sure that tagging *is* replacing a prison sentence; they are only likely to be more than marginal if tagging is used on a sufficient scale to enable prison places to be reduced. A few cells unused, here and there, will make no significant savings to prison costs—the Swedes made no claims on cost saving until they had been able to close a prison and abandon plans to build another. A German study, completed at the time that tagging was under active consideration concluded that if you want to save money in the criminal justice system *and* promote resocialisation, then tagging was not the answer. A reduction in sentence lengths would achieve those aims much more effectively.

Effectiveness is, of course, the other part of the equation. We have seen elsewhere that there are obvious ways of measuring this— successful completion is the most common short term measure but there is a wider range of possibilities, including:

- *Lower reconviction rates* These tend to be the ultimate goal—but also the most complex to assess, since the few studies which are available tend to be silent on at least one of the factors—predicted reconviction rate, speed of reconviction or quality of reconviction— which are really needed if confident judgements are to be made. Baumer and Mendelsohn (1990) recorded that 31.5 per cent of their study had an arrest, warrant or probation violation resulting in a court appearance in the year following monitoring; similar figures were recorded in Oregon (27 per cent) and Texas (32 per cent). The National Institute of Justice, in its much wider review, also concluded that recidivism had not been reduced.

  In Sweden, the three-year follow-up (Begler, 1999) discovered a small difference (two per cent) in favour of those who had been electronically monitored, as against a control group. Research figures from England and Wales suggest that tagging is 'offence-neutral', with reconviction rates broadly similar to those not tagged. Small and very specialised programmes can seem to produce better results—much more convincing evidence is needed. Only the Connecticut experience in the USA, which is referred to below, suggests that more may be achieved.

- *Unchanged reconviction rates—but a less costly sanction.* This is increasingly used as the most sustainable justification for expanded use of electronic monitoring but, again, it has to be tested against actual use. If the same offenders would do just as well on other, cheaper, community penalties, there are no cost savings. Tagging has to demonstrate an 'added value' component if it is to grow in use at any level in the sentencing framework.

Neither of these should detract from successful completion as a measure in its own right but, as we have seen, that is such a function of length of time tagged that we should look at claims based on this alone with some caution. It has been apparent for years, on a worldwide basis, that tagging for periods of one month or less should achieve a 95 per cent 'success' rate; and for up to two months, 90 per cent successful completion. Schemes such as the current Home Detention Curfew arrangements in England and Wales, which achieve this, cannot claim 'added value' for that alone. The current, expensive, selection and assessment procedure, which results in a very selective scheme could arguably be dropped—and the scheme much extended—with only a marginal impact on outcomes.

What we need to know is whether the period tagged—even if short—and the disciplined start it imposes has any impact on employment, family relationships or social behaviour. The impact on later reoffending might then be harder to measure, but may be much more significant.

The Connecticut experience

One of the most interesting experiments in which electronic monitoring has been introduced and where set policy and outcome measures were in use, was in Connecticut throughout the 1990s. The background starts in 1981, when legislation dismantled the parole system so that 'real time' had to be served by prisoners. A huge increase in the prison population followed and from 1985-1990 the state spent over $1 billion, building over 11,000 new prison places. By 1990, politicians and criminal justice officials were faced with the uncomfortable knowledge that this prison building effort had resolved neither their capacity or their credibility problems. They had, in fact, reached a point where, because of economic recession, the tax generated was no longer sufficient to keep the prisons they had got, let alone build more to cope with the unrelenting rise in numbers.

A Commission on Prison Overcrowding was appointed and proposed 'more effective sanctions for less money'—a full range of strictly enforced community based sanctions with prison as a defined penalty for breach. An Office of Alternative Sanctions (OAS) was set up to implement these, but the added twist to the story is that the enabling legislation was passed with a five-year 'sunset clause'. In other words, OAS had five years to demonstrate the programme worked effectively and managed risk to the community, or its funding would cease.

OAS moved swiftly into action and devised a wide range of alternative sanctions, of which electronic monitoring was one. Also included were:

- day treatment centres;
- community service schemes;
- day incarceration centres;
- drug treatment programmes; and
- a mixture of state and non-profit agency supervision.

750 offenders were dealt with in the first year; eight years later that had reached a of 150,000 with over 5,000 OAS-supervised offenders in the community at any one time. The outcomes were:

- just over 60 per cent completed successfully;
- just over 25 per cent were breached; and
- just under ten per cent committed a new offence while under supervision.

As far as longer term outcomes were concerned, an independent three-year follow up, using two comparable groups, found that OAS participants offended 30 per cent less than their counterparts—an exceptional result which, it was calculated, had diverted 40,000 offenders from prison and led to savings in both operating and capital costs of $619 million (Coleman *et al.*, 1998). By 1999, Connecticut's imprisonment rate was 17 per cent below the national average.

Electronic monitoring does not, of course, take all the credit for this remarkable result, which resulted in the 'sunset clause' being removed—the changes are now on the statute book without limitation. Tagging was only one of a number of options. And would all the OAS offenders really have gone to prison? Mr From Siconolfi, Director of the Justice Planning Unit, was candid, saying that while he thought two-thirds would have done so, the other third were 'arguably marginal'.

What the programme demonstrates, though, is that when tagging is integrated into a range of options; when it is managed well and sanctions are both clear and swiftly applied (the aim was to prosecute breaches in court the following day); then more effective penalties for less money are an achievable goal.

This approach—of using electronic monitoring as part of a wider approach and seeing if it can make a real contribution to overall results—is a much more realistic way of measuring the impact electronic monitoring has had, and the policy contribution it can make. Too much of the literature has concentrated on examining its record as an alternative to prison and although it can be argued that it was never presented just as a stand-alone option, many jurisdictions were seduced into believing that this was possible and it became a kind of bench mark against which schemes were measured.

It is difficult to understand why beliefs have been so slow to change. As early as 1990 Petersilia and Turner, in an authoritative study, had concluded

more supervision, without a substantive *treatment* component, evidently had little effect on offenders' underlying criminal behaviour.

A recent meta-analysis, which included an examination of the research on electronic monitoring found that, on average, electronic monitoring actually *increased* recidivism by about five per cent over comparable groups (Gendrau *et al.*, 2000). As a recent article (Latessa, 2000) noted, the question is not why this is the case, but rather why would we expect electronic monitoring, on its own, to have any effect on offender behaviour?

On both sides of the Atlantic, evidence-based practice, or 'what works' has become the centrepiece of criminal justice development, whether in prison programmes or in community alternatives. Put simply, four main principles that underlie effective criminal justice programmes have been identified:

- the risk principle (intervention should target higher-risk offenders);
- the need principle (intervention should be clearly linked to criminogenic need factors);
- the treatment principle (treatment should be behavioural in nature); and
- the responsivity principle (offenders, staff and programmes should be properly matched).

There is no reason to expect that, on its own, electronic monitoring can do more than provide short term and limited control. It certainly does not address the risks or needs that influence offender recidivism. Yet that does not mean that, as part of a wider programme, electronic monitoring cannot be incorporated into an approach that meets all these principles. Setting and enforcing curfews may be part of a wider risk management strategy—it needs, however, a risk reduction programme to be part of the overall approach if a really effective intervention is to be designed.

Within this kind of framework, tagging can find a secure base as a 'standard tool' in the criminal justice armoury, rather than the 'magic solution' which has, all too often been ascribed to it. That has already happened in Sweden and, intelligently used, there is no reason why it should not do so for much of western Europe, given the number of programmes now under way. At the same time, however, the outcome in policy terms is still hard to determine and any of the following scenarios is still possible:

- *Electronic monitoring will help to keep prison as the cornerstone of criminal justice policy.* Electronic monitoring blurs the boundaries when it is incorporated as a 'helping tool' at the end of a prison sentence. Growing enthusiasm for post-release tagging is easy to understand—it provides a way of easing the stark transition from captivity to freedom; there is some evidence that the curfew period may help repair family relationships which have been damaged by the period in custody; it enables large scale early release to be presented in a positive, risk-reduction, way rather than (as is so often the case) a convenient device to free up overcrowded prisons; and relatively short periods tagged produce good completion rates, even if longer term results are poor. But .... the wide availability of what is seen as a positive aspect of the prison sentence may simply make sentencers more ready to use prison and politicians to promote it. Prison has been a growth industry, world wide and with only a few exceptions, like Finland, for the whole of the last decade. Only in the last few years have most politicians started to admit, in private, that a continued growth is unsustainable and self- defeating. If electronic monitoring were to be the cause of continued growth in the use of custody—and that danger is still apparent—it would suffer an inevitable backlash;

- *Electronic monitoring will revitalise and strengthen the whole range of community penalties.* This is the opposite argument—and there is some evidence for it. Certainly in Sweden, as noted earlier, the Probation Service's involvement with electronic monitoring has given the service, and supervision in the community, a real boost. This is more than just a question of external public confidence in their ability to supervise properly, or internal staff confidence in their own ability to deliver effective programmes. It is about strengthening what most people consider to be a sensible, long- term approach—to tackle the causes of offending behaviour and work on them—without the short term problem of offenders being seen to 'get off' or walk free to pose an equal risk of reoffending. Seeing this translated into a change of sentencing practice is bound to be a long term affair and it will require an extraordinary effort from well resourced probation services if it is to be sustained. There are pitfalls, too, as one of the speakers at the 'Probation 2000' international conference pointed out. Will probation go:

  > from mere surveillance, to direct work with offenders, to treatment programmes .... and just back to more sophisticated surveillance? It cannot opt out—too many others are waiting in the wings to take it on.

Surveillance is growing rapidly and it is growing much faster than our ability to deal constructively with people.

(Stone, 2000)

Unrestricted growth of electronic monitoring without that constructive engagement remains the danger.

* *Electronic monitoring will compete with, rather than strengthen, community penalties—and will largely replace them.* This scenario, it seems to me, lay behind much of the early opposition to electronic monitoring from probation staff. Many minds were changed by the prospect of reduced use of custody, and the growing realisation, from pilot projects, that much positive work was helped, not hindered, by the curfew period. But there is still a real fear that the expansion of electronic monitoring, making it much more cost effective as numbers rise, will undermine the 'softer' community penalties, where breaches may be less clear cut and supervisors' discretion still leaves areas of uncertainty. There seems little evidence of this, so far, in North America, where the sheer length of time that electronic monitoring has been available would allow trends such as this to be evident; nor in Sweden, where the opposite effect has been observed. Community service orders, newly introduced, have captured part of the sentencing 'market' at the expense of electronic monitoring.

Poor targeting, poor results, a sustained run of poor publicity when tagged offenders are reconvicted—all these could still be influential in shifting perceptions from the currently positive image that tagging enjoys. Experience suggests they will have more impact than carefully argued research results. At the moment, the most reliable prediction would be that tagging will continue its slow growth as a court order, retaining a small 'market share' in sentencing terms—probably nearer three per cent than the current one-and-a-half to two per cent—and with major growth reserved for post-sentence (early release from prison) schemes. Current use of community penalties in England and Wales has been hugely influenced by the long, slow decline of the fine, from over a half to less than a third of all sentences. If lower unemployment and the resulting ability to pay fines can reverse this trend we may yet see changes in which external factors, rather than the intrinsic merit of electronic monitoring, are the most influential.

POLICY, SENTENCING AND RESEARCH

The quality and scope of the research currently being undertaken in England and Wales on both curfew orders and post-release home detention curfews should add considerably to the overall body of knowledge about how best to use these new tools. But will it have much impact on overall policy or the way in which individual offenders are sentenced? There are three reasons to doubt this.

First, most research confirms much of what we know, or suspect, already. The messages are often, overall, undramatic and common sense—the interest often lies in the detail and even then it frequently poses more questions than the answers it provides. The complaint made in the USA that, for a 'standard tool' there was a complete lack of serious research about whether it really works is not a new one but even when an attempt is made to remedy this we are not necessarily much further forward. A recent comprehensive study in Indiana (Roy, 1999) felt able to arrive at some definite conclusions. They were:

- successful completion of an electronic monitoring sentence is significantly related to previous offending history. First offenders are four times less likely to have the order revoked than those with previous convictions;
- sentence length is crucial. If the period electronically monitored is more than 90 days the probability of revocation increased by 4.6 times.

The author of the study conceded that previous research findings had repeatedly demonstrated these two predictors and, together with information on substance abuse, provided the key information. In short, it provided a well researched addition to the literature, but nothing new. Only much wider studies are likely to be able to look at aspects such as longer term success rates by offence type; or developing a more sophisticated offender typology which would help report writers and sentencers assess how the technology could be used most effectively. The view in the USA is that until matched pair samples using random assignment can demonstrate clear messages in these areas, the 'research deficit' will continue. Yet there are few here who feel the idea is practicable, now that schemes are well established.

So we have the latest Home Office research (Walter *et al.*, 2001) unable to help much—it records the views of practitioners and electronic monitoring staff that 'pattern' offenders could be particularly suitable, together with cases where 'custody was likely but inadvisable; and where other community penalties had been breached or were unsuitable' and, by way of counterbalance added, 'most felt curfew orders inappropriate for sex offenders, very violent offenders and where they raised domestic violence or child protection issues. Opinions were divided as to the value of tagging for offenders with chaotic lives and for substance misusers'. But the evidence to support these common sense views has yet to be found.

At the same time that this report was published (April 2001), the Home Office published three further studies. Two relate to the home detention curfew scheme (Mortimer 2001; Dodgson *et al.*, 2001); the third covers second-year reconviction results for the curfew order trials. Together, they make fascinating reading and provide as much information as any scheme in the world. But the key results are now part of an established pattern:

- successful completion rates of 90-95 per cent for short orders of up to two months;
- successful completion rates of 80 per cent for three to four-month orders;
- nearly 73 per cent of curfew order offenders were reconvicted of a further offence within two years of being sentenced. The impact of the post-release scheme was described as 'broadly neutral' in terms of reoffending;
- where schemes replaced prison (through early release) cost savings were said to be significant; and
- curfew orders as a sentence of the court were still underused.

With no real policy guidance, this is hardly surprising and there are no signs of early change.

Second, policy makers and sentencers tend to be much more influenced by short term pressures, media and public opinion. Research may have a longer term purpose in shaping a thoughtful debate, or advice to ministers, but decisions more often reflect immediate concerns, the latest high profile case, the immediacy of the next general election or the need to reassure the electorate. The civil servants in Canada, when asked why tagging was to be increased despite research (which the government itself had commissioned) indicating the opposite course of action, gave exactly the same answers as one would expect in the majority of western countries:—it gave a reassuring message to the public that they were doing something positive; it was cheaper than prison and, anyway, ministers had a mandate to spend public money in ways they thought most appropriate.

Third, electronic monitoring is only one of a new set of issues which beset the whole criminal justice system and, like the others with which it competes for attention, it cannot be considered in isolation. Among those which can be easily identified are the community justice movement, the managerialist agenda which is currently in vogue, and the prison 'growth industry' which has been equally apparent over the last decade.

A brief look at each illustrates neatly just how complex the current 'mix' of pressures and ideas has become.

The community justice movement, with its emphasis on improving the quality of community life at very local, street and estate level, is far from the nostalgic and romantic view of how communities used to be in quieter, earlier times. As Clear and Karp point out in *The Community Justice Ideal* much of it sprang from the lack of confidence people had in wider institutional solutions.

> In a quarter-century, the size, cost and potency of the justice apparatus has grown three to five times over, depending on how one counts the growth. Public confidence in the justice system is, if anything, less than when the growth began .... If the justice system were put up for a vote of confidence, the prospects would be dim.
>
> The movement of criminal justice towards community initiatives .... is a response to the common sense of dismay about community life. Criminal justice officials, sensing that confidence in their actions is slipping away, have sought a closer alignment with community members partly as a vehicle for increasing faith in justice practices. It must also be remembered that criminal justice practitioners are also members of the community. They feel some of the same disillusionment in official policies and they experience the same type of yearning for a better quality of community life.
>
> (Clear and Karp, 1999)

A wide range of imaginative and effective projects have resulted, including small scale 'crimestop' groups, joint police-probation-housing initiatives, special facilities for children whose fathers are in prison, mentoring schemes for adolescents. 'Habitat' groups where paid residents and offenders improve local amenities, schemes to 'pair' senior citizens with local offenders, after-school clubs .... all designed to meet a local need with local resources to reduce local offending. The hallmarks of the most successful schemes, say Clear and Karp, are that they do *not* replicate traditional measures; they are light years away from the politician's quick fix in their long term, preventive orientation and they are eminently flexible as they continue to evolve over time.

They are also a nightmare for researchers, difficult to control and therefore anathema to the centralising tendencies of governments, and frequently unorthodox in their definition of success or failure. But there are signs that, as a partial solution, they may have much to offer. Within this context, electronic monitoring may have only a limited appeal.

Managerialism, with its focus on output measures, performance indicators, strategic management and its own holy trinity of efficiency, effectiveness and economy is a world away from the community justice agenda. These, and the desire for a more consistent and co-ordinated response from criminal justice agencies (some of it long overdue) have resulted in a decade of almost constant tinkering, interspersed with bouts of much more significant change. Some has undoubtedly been for the better, although the impact has often been muted because no one initiative was ever allowed to consolidate its position before a raft of new ones arrived. But the result has been an emphasis on managing, rather than understanding or eradicating crime and, although electronic monitoring sits neatly within this framework, it may well not be to its long term advantage.

Finally, the prison growth industry—not an English or even a European phenomenon, but a worldwide one

> Prison populations are growing in many parts of the world. Updated information on countries included in the first edition [of the *World Prison Population List*, published by the Home Office Research, Development and Statistics Directorate] shows that prison populations have risen in 70 per cent of these countries; a similar pattern is evident in all continents'.
>
> (Walmsley, 2000)

It may be too early to draw conclusions but—again with Sweden as the honourable exception—countries with a high proportionate use of tagging have also a high and increasing prison rate. The USA, the obvious example, has the second highest rate of imprisonment in the world, at 680 per 1000; England and Wales, at 125 per 100,000 is well above the European average of 70 and Singapore, at 340 per 100,000 is around three times the average for South Eastern Asia.

The early hopes for tagging were that it would add something genuinely different to the bewildering range of options already available to criminal justice systems; that it might tackle parts of offending behaviour that other sentences had not reached. In terms of surveillance and control in the community—it does. This was linked to the hope that it might help teach offenders what Mary Tuck called 'the practice of virtue'—that is, of living crime free within their own communities (Tuck, 1991). But if all that tagging contributes is the translation of the techniques of prison into the world at large—and some see it, in policy terms, as exactly this—it will have reinforced the growth of prisons in a particularly unhelpful way.

None of this should suggest that conscious choices are necessarily being made. The shrillest voices may also be the loudest, but policy lurches on within a much more complex framework, not least because of the costs involved. The spectacular decline in the Russian prison population, with two enormous prison releases in successive years, owes everything to the frightening and unsustainable cost of keeping people locked up, rather than a newly enlightened approach to social and criminal justice.

The contribution that tagging might make is not so much a question of market share but of meeting specific needs. These include: offering sufficient control to meet public expectations in relation to deterrence and retribution; an element of incapacitation; sufficient flexibility to meet a wide range of offender needs, especially in conjunction with other programmes; and cost effectiveness. Sooner or later, it *must* also be able to demonstrate a measurable success in altering some aspects of offenders' behaviour and in reducing reoffending. Longer term development, especially with adult offenders, will be wholly dependent on its perceived ability to meet this specification.

YOUNG OFFENDERS

The use of tagging with young offenders has always been more controversial than with adults, and for good reasons. First, there could hardly be a more obvious 'label' than the tag and it would be virtually impossible to conceal it, for instance, during a school day that might involve sport or gymnasium activities. It would make a nonsense of the anonymity supposedly offered by the youth court. At the other end of the scale there were equal fears that it could just as easily be brandished among the young offender's peers as a status symbol and a way to achieve recognition of a most unhelpful kind. Above all, the fear has been that, in the very volatile world of adolescent offending, the tag would, even more than with adults, accelerate the path to custody by recording all breaches, however minor, leading to the inevitable return to court. Finally, the impact on already troubled families, for whom the tag might be equally intrusive, was uncharted territory and there was a proper degree of caution about adding yet more pressure.

For most jurisdictions, the arguments were sufficient to rule out any use with young offenders. A few schemes in the USA tried it, with the consent of parents, usually in conjunction with an intensive supervision programme. Most of the experience was too small scale to draw general conclusions (and in one case, the programme included a 'live-in' counsellor for an intensive period, so drawing any conclusion on the impact of the tag alone would have been impossible) but some cautiously optimistic noises were made about the way in which the tag enabled supervisors to use the short period monitored to 'get alongside' the young person and set in place more constructive programmes. These were usually employment or education focused and it was felt that the sheer quantity of contact in the initial stages enabled the 'quality' programmes later to start on a more secure footing.

Research in Indiana, which used a matched control group sentenced to 'ordinary supervision', reported good results with its youthful taggees. Those young people electronically monitored as a condition of supervision not only completed the supervision period satisfactorily more often (90 per cent as against 75 per cent) but reoffended less during the follow-up period (16.9 per cent against 25.9 per cent). The programme's primary aim seems to have been to reduce overcrowding in the state's juvenile detention centre but there were plans to extend it to a range of higher risk offenders once it was realised that the mix of fairly intensive supervision and tagging could be effective (Smylka and Selke, 1995).

The most recent verdict by Corbett on juvenile schemes in the USA is depressingly familiar, however: 'As with so much in the juvenile correctional field, little reliable scientific evidence is available on programme impact'. He goes on to cite an earlier study, which came to the eventual conclusion that 'two years of court supervision with community treatment (i.e. probation) is superior to any other sentence examined in this study, for eliminating and delaying recidivism'. (Corbett, 2000).

One more general finding however, is that the impact of electronic monitoring on family conflict has been rather less than expected. Indeed, some data suggests it may be positive in family terms. It helps towards producing a more structured lifestyle and, because its impersonal control replaces some of the family control over the young person, it can be significant in terms of reducing family conflict.

In England and Wales there has been much less caution about involving young offenders in electronic monitoring. During the pilot phase they were limited to 16- and 17-year-olds only, but in July 1997 Home Secretary Jack Straw announced that they would be made available in due course for 10-15 year olds and the Youth Justice Board has subsequently moved to implement this.

There are certainly welfare and health and safety concerns surrounding the tagging of children of this age, as well as more general concerns about likely effectiveness. It was decided that special care should be taken to explain the conditions of the order to parents as well as ensuring that those parents are available and present when the tag is fitted. There are special requirements on the contractors to ensure that certain standards are adhered to and that all employees are subject to security checks in line with Department of Health guidelines.

But .... who exactly are they *for*? The first two years of the pilot areas, when they were restricted to 16 and 17-year-olds, produced only 42 orders, just less than ten per cent of the total, and completion rates were—nor surprisingly—well below their adult counterparts. Research on ten to 15 year olds has not yet been published. At first there was some hope that, since it is possible to curfew in more than one location, it could be useful to make the school a curfew site where the offender was, as so often happens, a persistent truant. There are, however, real difficulties with this. The curfew period maximum is 12 hours per day and the night time curfew might well be more important; permission would be required from the school and there are real difficulties in trying to impose a reasonable curfew boundary on a site as large as a typical school.

Until more data about 10 to 15-year-olds is available, judgement will have to be reserved. For juveniles, however, very real doubts remain as to whether it will have a long term place in the battery of options available to courts. An extraordinary range of new initiatives has been ushered in by the new Youth Justice Board; courts and youth justice workers alike are having to work out how best to use a bewildering range of options, from specified activity orders, reparation requirements, action plans, parenting orders and many more. At this stage it seems unlikely that electronic monitoring will have a significant impact on the sentencing of young offenders, especially those under 16. Many would see that as wholly appropriate.

REFERENCES for *Chapter 7*

Baumter T and Mendelsohn R, *The Electronic Monitoring of Non-Violent Convicted Felons: An Experiment in Home Detention*, Indiana University 1990

Begler A-M, 'Intensiv-Överakning ned Elektronisk Kontroll', *BRA-Rapport* No. 4, Stockholm, 1999

Clear T and Karp D, *The Community Justice Ideal*, Boulder, Colorado and Oxford, Westview Press, 1999

Coleman P, Felton Green N J and Oliver G, 'Connecticut's Alternative Sanctions Programme' *Practitioner Perspectives*, October 1998, Washington, BJA

Corbett R.P, 'Juvenile Probation on the Eve of the Next Millennium,' *Perspectives*, Vol. 24 No. 4, Lexington, 2000

Dodgson K *et al.*, 'Electronic Monitoring of Released Prisoners', *Home Office Research Study*, No. 222, London, 2001

Gendrau P, Goggin G, Cullen FT and Andrews DA, 'The Effects of Community Sanctions and Incarceration on Recidivism', *Forum*, Vol. 12, No. 2 pp. 10-13, 2000

Latessa EJ, 'Incorporating Electronic Monitoring into the Principles of Effective Interventions', *JOM*, Vol. 13, No. 4 pp. 5-6, Fall 2000

Mortimer E, 'Electronic Monitoring of Released Prisoners', *Research Findings*, No. 139, London, Home Office, 2001

Persilia J M and Turner S, 'Comparing Intensive and Regular Supervision for High-risk Probationers', *Crime and Delinquency*, pp. 87-111, 1990

Roy S, 'An Analysis of the Exit Status of Adult Offenders in an Electronic Monitoring Home Detention Programme in Indiana', *JOM*, Vo. 12, No. 3, 1999

Smylka J and Selke W (Eds.), *Intermediate Sanctions: Sentencing in the 1990s*, Washington, NCJ, 1995

Stone C, 'Crime and Punishment: What the Future holds', Speech to Probation 2000 Conference, London, January 2000

Sugg D, Moore L and Howard P, 'Electronic Monitoring and Offending Behaviour', *Research Findings*, No. 141, London, Home Office, 2001

Tuck M, 'Community and the Criminal Justice System', *Policy Studies*, 12, pp..22-37, 1991

Walmsley R, 'World Prison Population List', second edn., *Research Findings*, No. 116, London, Home Office, 2000

Walter I, Sugg D, and Moore L, 'A Year on the Tag: Interviews with Criminal Justice Practitioners', *Research Findings*, No. 140, London, Home Office, 2001

CHAPTER 8

Wider Issues

Although a lively debate has occurred in the United Kingdom on the appropriate use of electronic monitoring, the potential impact of human rights legislation and the privacy of families, there have been few formal legal challenges. A recent Appeal Court case, challenging the legitimacy of breach proceedings, was recently won on procedural grounds but its effect will be on process, and on the direct evidence available to the court, rather than on principles or on wider practice. In some ways this is no surprise. The offender's consent is required before electronic monitoring equipment can be fitted as part of a curfew order and any later challenge would certainly be undermined by that consent (assuming that this was correctly and freely given after proper explanation by the sentencing court). Of course, consent to the order may well be based on the offender's perception that any alternative is likely to be worse. But consent it is, and it allows the operating authority to intrude into the offender's life and home in ways that would not otherwise be possible.

Equally, prisoners who wish to be considered for early release under the home detention curfew scheme have to apply for it, thus accepting the conditions which accompany the scheme. Prison service documents make it clear that, while most prisoners serving sentences of over three months and under four years are eligible, there is no automatic entitlement and the requirement on prisoners to 'work towards' satisfying the selection criteria is central.

Nevertheless, electronic monitoring has raised a whole raft of constitutional and legal issues in the USA and, while jurisdictions may be very different, it is worth looking at how they have been resolved, for the general picture which emerges.

TESTING THE SYSTEM: LEGAL CHALLENGES IN THE USA

Initial challenges to electronic monitoring centred quite specifically on constitutional rights—to privacy in particular—and whether tagging represented a 'cruel and unusual' punishment. Over the first few years it was established that conditions such as electronic monitoring had to meet four tests. They had to be:

- clear;
- reasonable;
- constitutional; and
- related to the protection of society and/or the rehabilitation of the offender.

The concept of 'reasonableness', which runs through all the interpretations of constitutional rights is important, as is the question of the 'diminished rights' of offenders, which allows broad discretion to sentencing authorities in establishing the conditions of release or of supervision programmes in which electronic devices are employed.

(US Dept of Justice, 1989)

The American Civil Liberties Union (ACLU) set down four major concerns when they reviewed the issue:

- the likely net-widening effect of electronic monitoring programmes (although they said they would have no complaint if it really did reduce the use of prison);
- Fourth Amendment issues (privacy and protection from unreasonable search and seizure). They recognised, however, that they were unlikely to be successful in litigation and the 1987 *Griffin v. Wisconsin* case (107.S.Ct.3164) removed most grounds when it authorised the warrantless, unannounced search of a probationer's home by his probation officer and police officers;
- general association and privacy rights. ACLU clearly saw tagging as the thin end of a larger anti-privacy wedge; and
- equal opportunity grounds. Tagging would discriminate against the poor and people with no homes or telephones.

This last issue is a real one and led to much soul searching in Sweden, too. Courts have consistently held that probationers and parolees can be charged fees, either for specific equipment or for supervision generally. A challenge that the rich get tagged and the poor get prison might well have some substance.

One view in the USA (Renzema and Skelton, 1990), is that general legal challenges will only really happen when the offender has nothing to lose. This is not the case with electronic monitoring, where one probable result of successful litigation would mean that the client goes to prison for the term for which electronic monitoring was meant to be the substitute. They concluded:

There are no realistic barriers to the use of electronic monitoring technology beyond the legal restrictions which already exist concerning the reasonableness of conditions of probation. Courts seem to have accepted the new technology (and the new probation methodology) without the need to create new legal principles or processes. Given a professionally administered program with properly operating equipment and procedurally efficient judicial and probation personnel, the use of electronic monitoring techniques for probationers, parolees and even pre-trial detainees is judicially acceptable as a proper method of supervision.

(Renzema and Skelton, 1990)

The qualifications in that last sentence are important in individual cases, but their broader point is widely accepted. Only the New York State Court of Appeals was more qualified in its approval—it ruled (*People v. McNair*, 4 April 1996) that, to be approved, conditions of probation such as electronic monitoring had to be 'fundamentally rehabilitative'. Since that was reversed by new enabling legislation soon afterwards, it seemed to be only a matter of process appeals, of faulty equipment and the like, which would detain the courts.

Until, that is, August 1999, when the Maryland Court of Appeals issued a ruling (*Bailey v. State*, 1999, WL 566756) which disallowed home detention as a condition of probation. This sent shock waves through the system—probationers are, after all, a major source of revenue to the monitoring companies—but its effect has, until now, been curiously muted. Six months later, numbers were down by only ten per cent. It is too soon to say whether this is the start of some legislative reappraisal, although in Ohio as well as Maryland, state legislatures are beginning to intervene. In Maryland, this was a direct result of at least two serious crimes committed by offenders under electronic monitoring supervision—a sobering reminder of just how fragile confidence can be, even when the system has been working well for years.

What has mostly happened have been challenges relating to quite specific issues. One revolved around the admissibility of evidence (Tony Ly. Texas R. App. P90) when it was contended:

- that the computer generated violation report, which constituted the evidence of breach of bail, was hearsay; and
- that the monitoring system's computer printout was not shown to be reliable and that the officer testifying did not understand the scientific theory of the equipment.

Neither was accepted by the court and, indeed, more general ruling on scientific evidence allows it 'if it has achieved general acceptance in the relevant scientific community'.

A good deal of time has been spent on deciding whether violating the conditions of post-release monitoring (under parole or other early release schemes) constitutes an 'escape'. Some states certainly prosecute on this basis and in Texas, for instance, the implications are significant. In *Choice v. State* (Tex. Cr.App. 1991) a detainee was released from prison on 'pre-parole' status which included a condition that he not leave his residence except under certain conditions and that he submit to electronic monitoring. After several violations, his parole officer might have revoked his parole status and returned him to prison, but instead, the prosecutor charged him with a felony escape. Because he had two previous felonies this would have earned a 25-year minimum sentence. He did, fortunately, win his appeal.

(Skelton, 1999)

Other states adopt a more logical rule that an escape charge can only be based on violation of a condition that actually constitutes 'custody'—and since electronically monitored home detention does not approximate to prison, the argument ends there.

It is unlikely, however, that legal issues have gone away entirely and the advent of continuous tracking, whether by satellite or by other systems, is already producing some debate on issues of:

- rights to privacy under the Fourth Amendment. The potential for lawsuits alleging violation of third party privacy rights is also seen as considerable;
- liability of supervisors for failure to respond to known violations, or lawsuits alleging liability for injuries to third parties arising from equipment failures or programme management; and
- vendor liability. This is a subsection of the previous issues but one in which a number of cases have been settled. As Skelton (1995) noted: 'people who have been victims of crimes committed by persons being monitored have brought actions for money damages against agencies supervising the detainees or against the vendors of the electronic monitoring equipment. We may never actually see an appellate case because the lawsuits tend to be settled before trial ....'.

Skelton added a fourth 'unresolved issue'—unintended, collateral or unanticipated consequences of electronic monitoring status—adding wryly that these, by definition, are unpredictable—and that the imagination of the American plaintiff's bar knows no bounds.

Satellite tracking has (at this stage) only had one case decided at federal level, when a bailee asked to be monitored in this way, rather than by home detention curfew, to allow him greater freedom of movement. The court instituted a month-long review and investigation into satellite monitoring, to evaluate the system's practicability and limitations. It was satisfied with the result (and acceded to the alleged offender's request) and, commenting on the decision, the *Journal of Offender Monitoring* noted:

Challenging the form of monitoring should become more straightforward as the factors for setting release conditions are clarified. That an in-depth study was undertaken on the system and was noted in this decision may be helpful to future challenges to this form of monitoring. A point not to be overlooked, however, is that (the defendant) was required to pay the costs associated with the satellite system. A defendant who wishes to utilise the satellite system rather than another form of monitoring system should be prepared to pay for it.

(Cook, 1999)

PRIVATISATION

Like private prisons, electronic monitoring brings with it some of the core dilemmas about allowing the profit motive to become part of the criminal justice process. In a burgeoning industry—and a highly competitive one—there are always likely to be contractors who do not reach the standards required and, with private prisons demonstrating the problems in their sharpest form, opponents of privatisation have rarely been without material to further their case. Yet, a decade of experience has shown that contract compliance, properly monitored and enforced, can deal with such criticism successfully. Like the state sector, there are good and bad private prisons. How you deal with the problems they produce is the key issue and many would argue that the contractual arrangements with the private sector make problem solving somewhat easier.

Electronic monitoring has had private sector involvement from the very beginning and it now has a wide variety of public-private partnership arrangements. The three main models are:

- *wholly private.* The contractor provides the equipment and the monitoring centre, has front line staff fitting equipment and dealing with offenders on a day to day basis; and undertaking court work for breach and violation. The role may also include the collection of designated fees from offenders;

- *hybrid.* There are several variations, the most common of which is for the contractor to provide the equipment and the 24-hour monitoring service; and for the probation or parole authority to fit the tags and home monitoring units, to undertake all the day-to-day supervision and to remain responsible for the court process. This brings with it the need to train probation staff in unfamiliar roles, so in England and Wales the decision was taken to extend the contractor's role. Here, the companies involved undertake *all* the directly related monitoring work. Their staff fit the tags and the home monitoring unit and retain direct contact throughout the monitoring period. For 'stand-alone' orders (i.e. with no other Probation Service involvement) they therefore have sole responsibility. For orders made in conjunction with other forms of supervision such as a probation order or period of licence, they have to work closely with the statutory service—and early experience of this front-line partnership has generally been good. In Scotland, there are slight variations in that prosecution of breaches relating to electronic monitoring are passed over to the Procurator Fiscal (the state prosecution authority) and minor changes of this kind are likely to occur as jurisdictions move from small scale pilots to much larger schemes; and

- *supplier only.* Sweden is unusual in insisting that, apart from equipment supply, the Probation Service undertake complete operating responsibility, including after-hours calls, response to violations, equipment fitting and checking. This is, in many ways, a logical extension of their approach that electronic monitoring cannot be used effectively on its own—it must be part of a programme of treatment, for which the Probation Service is wholly responsible. The Probation Service therefore assumes equal responsibility for what is seen as the adjunct to the main purpose of the order.

Minor variations of all three models are evident around the world, with the choice of options often dependent on a mixture of cost, size and political considerations. Because equipment is getting more complex, more sensitive and therefore more difficult to install and maintain it seems likely to me that the trend is towards more involvement by contractors. How it works in practice is, perhaps, best explained by describing one such operation, as below.

Case study: Premier Monitoring Services

Premier Monitoring Services is responsible for electronic monitoring in two of the four English regions—a huge swathe of country which includes London and the Midlands, East Anglia and the whole of Wales—and has 150 staff servicing the operation, from eight bases. The sheer geographical spread means that most front line staff work from home, in the area they cover, but fluctuating demand means a high degree of mobility is required if Home Office requirements about initial visits, follow-up calls and response times are to be met. Staff also have to be available regionally for court cases—the company is responsible, under its contract, for all breach cases, and the costs of prosecuting offenders. This, in itself, adds a new dimension to the public-private relationship. The criticism about the private sector wanting to fill all spaces regardless of suitability (often levelled against private prisons) clearly does not apply in the electronic monitoring field. Too many breaches, especially 'not guilty' pleas where barristers are required to prosecute, is the quickest road to unprofitability. Equally, there are stringent audit procedures (reinforced by Home Office 'fines' for non-compliance) to ensure that violations are properly recorded and dealt with. The commercial impetus is very much to get offenders through orders, successfully.

The hub of the operation, however, is the central control room at Norwich. Premier took over the original pilot project contractors, Geografix, and in doing so have retained staff from the very beginning of the scheme. This has given them an enormous advantage in terms of the experience that has been accumulated in a business that, for all its technical wizardry, still depends hugely on the quality and clarity of contact between offenders and contractor's staff. In a large, airy, open plan room staff work in groups of five in an atmosphere that, at first sight, looks far removed from a frenetic operations room or a large commercial call centre. Yet it is, in reality, a mixture of both. Operations planning requires a daily schedule of induction visits, where equipment and the tag itself have to be fitted and the conditions explained. These may be known in advance, for home detention curfew cases—but they may, equally, come from courts in respect of curfew orders and be completely unpredictable.

Tasks like these are allocated geographically to the 'responsible officers' who undertake them and also make the follow up visits when it appears that violations have been recorded. The first check is always a telephone call from the control centre, to determine whether the offender really *is* home and these are made within minutes of the occurrence. Explanations ranging from taking a bath, just going to the bottom of the garden, a bus being a few minutes late or apparent equipment malfunction are scrupulously recorded—it is clear that patterns soon show whether an attempt to circumvent the requirements is being made—and decisions are taken on where follow up calls are needed or where 'level one' violations should be logged and warning letters sent.

In the early days, when numbers were small, monitoring staff quickly built up a rapport with offenders and the friendly but fair voice on the telephone became, for some, an additional source of help and advice at times of crisis. With 1,500 offenders a day to supervise this is no longer possible but the interaction between the offender and the unseen voice of authority and control remains important. Staff checking by telephone can call up all previous occurrences on screen as they talk to offenders and when, as in one case, the 'I've been in the bath—that must have been the problem ' excuse is used once too often they can point out that this apparent new obsession with cleanliness is a cause for concern—and that a random visit will be made to reinforce the requirements.

Most of the 'testing' by offenders comes in the early part of the order and a firm response from both telephone and field staff then means that compliance later is much improved. Most curfews are for night-time periods, so staff on shifts when the curfew begins and ends (mostly 7.00 p.m. and 7.00 a.m.) have a hectic time. Daytime shifts are correspondingly quieter but specialist court and administrative staff are on hand, the in-house audit team are ensuring contract compliance and workload planning is being continuously updated. It all adds up to a busy and purposeful scene—but so far removed from the difficult and occasionally dangerous business of supervising 1,500, often serious, offenders that it is easy to forget the realities of the messy, chaotic and sometimes very delinquent lives that are being monitored.

Andy Homer, now responsible for an operation that has expanded hugely from the early pilot scheme in Norfolk that he first managed, has no difficulty in keeping in touch with reality, however. To him come queries on the permissible use of discretion—just what is a 'reasonable excuse?'; the legality of some court decisions; the assessment of risk; requests for unusual variations in curfew hours .... in short, all the non-standard problems that cannot be dealt with elsewhere. But he holds to the 'Norfolk Principle' he established in the very beginning: good, clear communication with offenders, courts (and sentencing magistrates in particular), police, and supervising probation officers makes the difference between an ordinary and a well run scheme. Electronic monitoring crosses so many boundaries—not just the commercial and statutory ones, but professional ones, too—that one could never argue with this. Standards, in absolute terms, are set by the Home Office. It is the way they are met that determines the quality of the scheme.

Despite occasional concerns (newspaper reports about identification of offenders, to ensure the right prisoner was actually wearing the tag) and well publicised hiccups (a single incident, in which a tag was fitted, inexplicably, to an artificial limb, achieved world-wide and gleeful media coverage), confidence in the operation of tagging and private sector involvement is high in England and Wales. Credibility with sentencers, in particular, is enhanced by swift and consistent breach action and, although the growth in Curfew Orders as a sentence of the court remains relatively slow there is no evidence that it is privatisation that has held it back.

That confidence could be fragile, of course. Texas, Illinois, Utah and New Mexico have all experienced cases in which high profile murder and rape offences have been committed by offenders who were being electronically monitored. When, as happened in all these states, it was discovered that monitoring equipment had not recorded the violation, or that a slow response to a violation had contributed to the situation, electronic monitoring schemes are in trouble, whether the expectations of what they might have done are realistic or not. In some cases, the schemes have been stopped altogether.

The commercial pressures which fuel good practice (a well run scheme in one state or country is the best way of achieving new business elsewhere) also lead to unrealistic expectations, however. It is arguable that over-selling, and the unrealistically high expectations which followed, were one of the main causes of the unexpectedly slow development of electronic monitoring. The same hype is already evident in relation to satellite tracking systems, with the added burden of much larger development costs and—potentially- a smaller market because of unit costs. The private sector is inextricably linked to electronic monitoring and it would be disappointing, to say the least, if the same pattern were to be repeated.

REFERENCES for *Chapter 8*

Cook P, 'Legal Developments', *JOM*, Vol. 12, No. 1, Winter 1999

Renzema M and Skelton D, *The Use of Electronic Monitoring by Criminal Justice Agencies*, Report No. OJP-89-M-309, Washington DC, NIJ, 1990

Skelton D, 'Appellate Litigation involving the Electronic Monitoring of Offenders: a Ten-Year Retrospective', *JOM*, Vol. 12, No. 3, Summer 1999

US Dept of Justice, *EM in Intensive Probation and Parole Programs*, Washington DC, 1989

CHAPTER 9

A Look to the Future

Electronic monitoring is at the forefront of what is becoming known as the 'techno corrections' industry—that is, the process by which criminal justice or corrections agencies take advantage of the whole range of new technologies to cut costs, enhance supervision, improve detection or reduce risk. For technology has not only transformed crime, it is transforming the way we deal with it, too.

Two major reports from the Crime Prevention Panel of the Office of Science and Technology (OST), *Just around the Corner* and *Turning the Corner* (both published in 2000), have spelt out three positive ways in which new technology can reduce both crime and the fear of crime:

- by directly applying it to crime problems, either as an aid to detection (DNA analysis, for instance) or by increasing the security of people and property (CCTV);
- by designing secure products which reduce opportunities for theft and criminal misuse. As *Turning the Corner* notes, 'New technology will allow smaller, more anonymous groups or individuals to commit crimes previously beyond their means …. quickly and without trace against targets at both a national and international level'; and
- indirectly, by being universally available across society, strengthening communities and reducing social exclusion.

What was missing was a fourth category—new technology as an aid to reducing *re*-offending, which could have almost as great an impact. Technology can do much more than improve data collection and analysis, important though that is. Surveillance and control can also be much more specific than the more general coverage provided by CCTV. Targeting individuals, either those who have already offended, or those who may be expected to, is now on the agenda. It also, of course, has profound possibilities for more ominous and destructive uses, in terms of individual freedoms, intrusions into family and private matters and social control of both offenders and law abiding citizens alike.

Any glimpse into the future, therefore has to grapple with some uncomfortable questions as well as a seductive array of technological marvels. There is a need to explore legal and ethical issues before the use of new technologies becomes commonplace; an equal need to consider levels of intrusiveness before new systems allow them to escalate without check. Who is going to control technological control—and how?

Electronic tagging, satellite tracking systems and biometrics—the science of computerised identification of living individuals, using physiological characteristics—are all available now. Pharmacological and neurobiological developments, including genetic risk assessments, are certainly not far away. All have undoubted virtues as well as the capacity to become villains, so this is not a one sided debate. But the opportunity to work out the principles on which they should be used; to exploit the advantages without being trapped and ultimately damaged by the disadvantages, has to be grasped now.

Electronic tagging—now, technologically speaking, old hat—is a good place to start. It has shown the potential for problems in sharp relief, yet it has also—through becoming widespread and well established—set a kind of baseline on the continuum of surveillance and control. In offering a choice to offenders (whose consent is effectively if not formally needed) and a generally accepted positive outcome (reduced use of prison) it has established a *climate* in which other forms of control can flourish. Has it also opened the floodgates?

So far, as this book has demonstrated, the advance of tagging has been curiously muted, not least because of its inability—usually—to deliver on the two promises made for it: that it would increase public safety by imposing strict controls on offenders, with the certainty of detection if they were broken, and a reduction in the (expensive) use of prison beds where (cheap) community penalties involving tagging could be used. Better targeting, a wider range of schemes and learning from research should improve on that, but in the meantime technology is pushing hard at other boundaries.

Satellite tracking, using GPS (ground position by satellite) signals, is the obvious next step and is already in use, albeit on a very limited basis. 'Real time' tracking produces equally real problems, however, including the difficulty of investigating false alerts, the management of the huge quantity of data produced by such schemes, signal strength (and signal loss) and battery life. Sooner or later, these will be resolved and the clamour for such systems, already apparent from both politicians and judges, will have to be faced. We need, before then, to address one central, urgent question: if we set an offender free to roam in the community, yet also feel we must track him or her everywhere, what are we trying to do? If the risks are so great, why on earth are they being run outside prison walls? If the answer is that they have reached the end of an imposed sentence and there is no power to hold them any longer (and these are the only circumstances in which I can think it would currently be justified) then post-release tracking is likely to be too small, in numbers, to be commercially viable. It is also likely to be effective only for relatively short periods, whereas some of the highest-risk offenders—paedophiles—characteristically have long gaps between recorded offences. Any attempt to use GPS systems for less risky cases just because they are available ought to be resisted. Cost alone may make satellite tracking impracticable for large numbers of offenders, but that was said in the early days of 'ordinary' tagging, too. The verdict on tagging must be highly conditional at this stage, but decisions about second generation systems will certainly be taken before all the lessons from early mistakes have been learned.

Biometrics, at least, has the possibility of being rather less intrusive. Voice recognition systems which, through telephone contact, allow both identity and location to be checked, are simple, relatively cheap and do not require any equipment to be worn. But they are less effective at curfew enforcement, for instance and seem at this stage to be more appropriate for large scale use in lower-risk cases, and to cut the cost of supervision. Like tagging, biometrics applications (which include recognition via palm prints and retinas as well as the voice) are a useful tool which can enhance supervision or control, rather than operate independently. Current criminal justice usage includes the booking and management of prison visits (Ford, 2000) as well as Probation Service and youth justice supervision.

Biometrics also provides us with a grim reminder that new technology can be closely linked to the committing of crime, as well as to efforts to provide a solution to it. Professor Ken Pease, a member of the task force which produced the Office of Science and Technology reports referred to earlier, points out that—so far—innovation has always disregarded crime consequences and we tend to reap a crime 'harvest' which retro-solutions only ever partially solve. He gives the example of auto-teller cash machines in South Africa. Faced with a surge of assaults on people who were using the machines, and who were forced to reveal their PIN code to enable offenders to withdraw money, banks introduced machines using biometrics. Now, only a thumb print would act as a security device. The next act in this unhappy drama was a spate of thumbs being chopped off, to enable criminals to retain access to this source of easy money. Modifications had to be swiftly implemented to ensure that the machines would not accept a thumb print unless a pulse could also be detected (Pease, 2000).

Pease likens the race between the use of new technology to deter crime and its exploitation for illegal activity, to the arms race, where each side leapfrogs the other and the whole process escalates out of control. Satellite tracking is already in the process of escalating the potential surveillance and control of individual offenders—it can determine which side of the road they are on, which building they have entered, how fast they are travelling if they are in a car—and it can enforce 'exclusion zones' in order to prohibit an offender from approaching a victim's home, or a school, for instance. The possibilities are awesome, for both use and misuse. Appropriate, principled usage, as well as effective usage, has to be given serious consideration now, *before* it becomes widespread.

The component parts of ever more sophisticated systems, whether in tracking or biometrics, are already in the wings. So, too, are pharmacological and neurobiological developments which may also have a role in reducing offending. So-called 'wonder drugs', used to control behaviour in the mentally ill, are now being considered for use with offenders. Drugs that affect the level of brain neurotransmitters are used to help treat drug abuse; the relationship between the neurotransmitter serotonin and violent crime is also under particular scrutiny. It is only a matter of time before drugs are developed to control neurobiological processes—and we have, before then, to consider whether they are legitimate tools to manage violent offenders, or perhaps to try and prevent violence.

The same issues will also arise from gene management technologies (already widely used in agriculture) and work on profiling the genetic roots of human behaviour. Researchers in the USA are already discussing the development of risk assessment tools that use genetic profiles to warn of a propensity to addiction or to violence. When will courts, knowing they are available, start to insist on having them before sentence? How accurate can they be in dealing with individuals? How long before we start sending people to prison, or keeping them there, because of a *potential* danger to society?

I have allowed myself this brief digression beyond the sphere of electronic monitoring because it illustrates the issues which electronic monitoring has already placed before us. And electronic monitoring, with its immediate possibilities, provides a ready made launch pad for other developments. It is when we start to relate techno-corrections in general to sex offenders in particular that we come face-to-face with the most demanding and uncomfortable questions about desirable ends and difficult means. Predatory sex offenders pose more difficulties than almost any other group in terms of managing risk. What if we were to track them by satellite, if not for life, for long periods? And what if they were to be implanted with a small computer chip which measured the hormone levels which control sexual arousal? And, again, what if ....their tag were programmed to stun them, momentarily, if those hormone levels rose beyond a predetermined mark, or they came too close to a school or a house with a location alarm?

The technology to take this forward is not a problem. Our willingness to sanction this level of surveillance and control, however, may well be. Do we care if technology is used only for incapacitation or control, or do we want it to enhance rehabilitation?

The *potential* for the abuse of power, whether by the state or by criminal justice agencies, cannot simply be dismissed. There is a genuine debate to be had about the need to maintain public safety and the equally important need to preserve essential freedoms. Techno-corrections are set to expand, and so will the net of social control. Systems will get better—and cheaper, too. Dealing with social and behavioural problems in the name of public safety is going to be a siren song. The debate centred on electronic monitoring and criminal justice policy is much wider than reoffending rates, prison overcrowding or enhancing community supervision. We will have to find a framework within which values and ethical issues are considered and set down; in which the advantages and disadvantages of new technologies are clearly understood; and in which policy makers and legislators make clear how they are going to minimise the threats to general social control when they propose new technologies for dealing with offenders.

We would do well to remember the conclusion of the book *Nation of Meddlers*:

> The more we ask government to meddle in the lives of others, the closer we get to creating an apparatus that will, in all likelihood, eventually meddle in our own.
>
> (Edgley & Brissett, 2000)

CONCLUSION

Over the next few years decisions will need to be made, all over Europe, about the longer term future for electronic monitoring and other forms of technology as a means of supervising offenders. Some of these decisions will follow pilot schemes; others the need to renew contracts in the light of substantial operating experience. All of them will have to take account of much wider considerations than the technology itself—policies on law and order in general and sentencing in particular, the size and cost of prison populations, public acceptance and, perhaps, commercial pressures.

What advice can be given to anyone who has to weigh up the options, to inform politicians, or to decide on resource priorities? A number of messages are clear:

- technology has demonstrated its capacity to be a reliable and useful *tool* in offender supervision. It is not a programme in its own right and it is a false economy to use it as such. The conclusion that e.m is broadly 'offence neutral'—that it does not affect reconviction rates either way—is well documented. Reducing reoffending is linked to well targeted programmes of supervision in which technology can be used to provide 'added value'—a higher level of surveillance to reduce risk, or a more disciplined framework in which other programmes can take effect.

- the key to cost effective use is good targeting. The potential for e.m to increase, rather than decrease, prison populations in low-risk cases is also well known and discussion with sentencers here indicates that this may still become an unintended consequence of extended use of e.m in England and Wales.
- large scale use is likely to be directed towards early release from prison schemes, where e.m is a useful device for controlling prison numbers administratively. Experience suggests that it is cheaper—and just as effective—to reduce the length of time served in prison, but e.m makes early release more acceptable, politically and publicly, by promising an orderly transition from custody to freedom.
- other new developments, such as voice verification and satellite tracking are technically viable and available. Their use, too, needs to be properly targeted to ensure appropriate use and it is the issue of 'niche' marketing which ought to be focus of attention, now. Different technologies do different jobs. Ensuring a proper match between equipment and the kind of supervision which is most effective is essential if the longer term future of technology as an aid to offender supervision is to be assured.

Well used, technology can enhance supervision and increase confidence in the range of community based sentences of which it could become an integral part. Using it selectively and sensibly remains crucial—too much use with low-risk offenders risks net widening and accelerating their path to prison; too much use with high-risk offenders sets them up to fail and provides only the illusion of risk reduction to the community. The point that surveillance is growing much faster than our ability to deal with it constructively is a real one. We can only keep an effective balance by careful targeting.

Finally, the issue of social control, and the extent to which ever more sophisticated forms of surveillance can contribute to this, needs to be the subject of a much more open debate than has occurred so far. The fear of crime and the need to supervise offenders in the community represent a back door through which increasingly intrusive systems can be introduced. Offenders, those with mental health problems, the confused elderly, have already been identified as target groups. How soon before the criteria are widened?

The offender field offers users of electronic monitoring two vital opportunities. First, a way of *integrating* a range of options into supervision which is more than mere surveillance—which seeks to understand and remedy the causes of offending behaviour and aims to result in safer communities for us all. Second, an opportunity to explore and understand the potential and the limitations of these powerful new tools; to ensure that their use is not disproportionate and an affront to human rights, and to contribute to the well-informed public debate which we badly need.

•　　•　　•

POSTSCRIPT

While writing this book I came across an advertisement for 'Bluetooth' technology, which uses short range wireless technology to provide links between mobile computers, mobile phones and other portable hand held devices. Promising high data speeds over fast simple and secure wireless connections, with none of the cabling normally required, it is currently operable at distances of up to ten metres—but is set to develop a 100-metre range before too long. The advertisement explained the process:

> The key component is a tiny electronic module that contains a complete low power wireless transmitter and receiver .... One Bluetooth device can work simultaneously with up to seven others and up to 80 such devices can co-exist in the same room without interference .... The mobile phone sector is expected to be the first area for the widespread introduction .... in the longer term, Bluetooth interfaces will be added to a very wide range of computer products and industrial equipment as well as domestic appliances and portable consumer products. Bluetooth wireless technology could be fitted to more than 900 million products in five years!
>
> (*Guardian*, 2 October 2000)

Intrigued by the possibilities, and by the promise that this was an 'open specification' which could be incorporated into products without paying a licence fee, I telephoned Ericsson Ltd to talk to the product development section. What would the applications be, I asked, in the field of electronic monitoring of offenders? There were two answers, both cheerfully and honestly explained. The first was 'none'—electronic monitoring for offenders was far too uncommercial and unviable a market for a device which had, literally, the whole world of portable equipment in its sights. It was unlikely that such a specialised application would command any of the highly expensive research and development time needed to explore the practicalities and potential. The second answer was simply this, 'It may not be on anyone's priority list now, sir, but when it is, your book is certainly going to be out of date. Anyone trying to plan for a settled framework .... well, that's not how it is. Your world, as well as everyone else's, will be turned upside down'.

It looks as if being clear what we want electronic monitoring to achieve; the limits of control and surveillance we are prepared to sanction and an understanding of the balance between public safety and private freedoms will soon come into even sharper focus. Now is the time to engage with the issues.

REFERENCES for *Chapter 9*

Edgley J and Brissett W, *Nation of Meddlers*, Westview Press, 2000

Ford T, 'Video Imaging and Biometric Identification at Doncaster', *All Points Bulletin*, Vol. 6 No. 4. , Florida, Wackenhut Corrections Corp, 2000

Office of Science and Technology, *Just Around the Corner*, London, Office of Science and Technology Crime Prevention Panel, March 2000

Office of Science and Technology, *Turning the Corner*, London, Office of Science and Technology Crime Prevention Panel, December 2000

Pease K, 'The Future of Crime and Criminology', Address in British Society of Criminology, London, June 2000.

Appendix: Electronic Monitoring Technologies

The electronic monitoring of offenders is no longer the simple process of enforcing a home curfew, although that remains the most common technology in use. Methods and systems have grown considerably in the last few years and now fall into one of three main groups:

- home monitoring systems;
- voice verification; and
- satellite tracking.

Home monitoring systems themselves have become much more sophisticated since early curfew programmes provided evidence of their reliability and usefulness. The basic system remains the most common, however; in this, the offender wears a small electronic device, or 'tag' on the wrist or ankle. The tag acts as a small transmitter and a monitoring unit, or receiver, is located by and connected to the normal home telephone line. The tag is worn 24 hours a day—at work, school, home or during any activities—and sends a constant signal so that it can always confirm whether the wearer is keeping to the limits set by the court. These are usually the confines of the home, and set curfew hours determine when the offender has to be there. The range of the equipment is variable and so can be set to accommodate different sized properties.

The signal sent by the tag is relayed to a 24-hour monitoring centre, whose computers are programmed to know when the offender is supposed to be at home. They can also detect any attempt to tamper with the equipment, including the tag itself. Depending on agreed procedures, staff are then alerted by pager, telephone or fax to check on the offender—by telephone or by a home visit—before any action is taken to deal with the violation of the conditions.

Most tamper detection technologies can, eventually, be overcome, so manufacturers now use multiple technologies in both the transmitter and strap assemblies. The tags themselves have grown steadily smaller over the years and are now little bigger than a diver's watch. Secure fitting is much more obtainable from placement around the ankle, rather than the wrist, so most schemes insist on ankle fitment, other than in exceptional circumstances. This *continuous monitoring* remains the most commonly used system.

Random, or programmed systems do the same job, but using a pre-set checking mechanism of periodic checks according to an agreed schedule of activities. While continuous monitoring schemes concentrate on one location only (normally the offender's home), programmed systems can be set for multiple locations, with each location 'defined' by its corresponding telephone number. Normally only land-line telephones are acceptable, since mobile telephones would, of course, defeat the object of being certain about the offender's location. However, where a land-line is not installed—or in very rural areas—GSM technology allows mobile phone units, fitted with special anti-tamper devices, to be used. These were only licensed, after special testing, towards the end of 2000, so little is known as yet of their effectiveness. The security of the tag and its strap—and their ability to alert the monitoring centre. If any attempt to remove or tamper with them is experienced—is the main method of ensuring that the right person has been checked. But other options are also available, including video telephones for visual identification, or 'voiceprints' (of which more below) to ensure the integrity of the check. For those jurisdictions which require abstinence from alcohol as part of the conditions, home monitoring equipment can also: either measure the breath alcohol level of the participant or indicate that it is very likely alcohol has recently been consumed—in which case a home visit to test is likely. Clearly, double checks of the types noted above are needed to ensure the right breath goes into the alcometer. Nor is the equipment free of technical problems, if operators views are heard. But remote testing of this kind, for drug or alcohol use, is clearly an important early warning signal and all home monitoring systems are likely to develop these additional options in due course.

Voice verification offers rather different possibilities. On its own, it has the twin advantages of cheapness and flexibility, though it may also be incorporated in other options. A voiceprint, like a fingerprint, is unique to an individual and can be checked to a very high level of accuracy. An 'enrolment' process is essential, so that a voice template can be created for the individual offender. This is a short, simple process that consists of repeating a number of words or phrases (often, pairs of numbers) that are then used in different ways during the daily checks.

Depending on the degree of risk, or supervision required, a contact schedule will be agreed. The offender goes to the designated phone at that location and calls a 'free phone' number. The computer responds by asking for words or numbers to be repeated and can check, within seconds, whether the right person, from the right location, has called. Normal checking frequency is three or four times a day—but high-risk offenders may have to check in more often. The active part which the offender has to play is a powerful (and intrusive) reminder that he or she is under supervision. The system deals easily with multiple locations, so checks can be made at home, at work, at a drug treatment centre or—indeed—anywhere else where a telephone is available.

Voice verification does not act as a curfew device, in the way the tag does. But no special hardware is required, there are no bracelets to be worn and, if random checks are needed, a pager can be issued to the offender to instruct him or her to call the monitoring centre at any time. As with all monitoring systems, supervising officers can be notified within minutes if all is not well and the offender has either failed to respond—or been located in the wrong place.

Voice verification offers a simple and cost effective addition to community supervision, rather than a replacement for it. For low-risk cases it may save time and money by having some checks made by telephone rather than by personal contact and the Voice Track Corporation in the USA had over 10,000 completed cases to demonstrate this. The first European trials, in the Kent Probation Area (and later extended to London and North Wales) have extended this with high-risk offenders where it seems to offer very effective additional checks as part of an overall supervision plan.

Satellite tracking seems to offer the best of all worlds—the ability to determine the exact whereabouts of the offender at any time through continuous monitoring. The offender not only wears the traditional transmitter, but also carries (or wears, through a waist belt) a portable receiver/tracking unit. The location of the unit is determined by data transmitted from Global Positioning Satellites. The technology has been in both military and civil use for a number of years and will be familiar to yachtsmen, mountaineers and a wide variety of commercial users who need to monitor vehicle movements, for instance. It offers not only location data, but the ability to offer 'exclusion zones', where an audible alarm warns both the offender and the monitoring centre if, for example, the offender goes within a mile of a victim's house. For very high-risk, repeat offenders, including some of domestic violence, this offers a welcome additional degree of protection.

But .... satellite tracking has not had an easy start. It is very expensive, compared with other forms of electronic monitoring—and thus less likely to be used on any scale by hard pressed correctional services. Technical difficulties are by no means resolved, either. Battery weight and life are improving but signal interference is still an issue, and so is the management of tracking systems, which produce mountains of data. Most people involved believe that the technical difficulties can and will be overcome; whether cost considerations and system management will be so amenable remains to be seen. Alternative developments include *urban locator systems*, which use a network of radio towers and cellular telephone technology. Tracking whether by satellite or not, is still presented as the future of electronic monitoring and its promise to monitor both time and place for individual offenders is a powerful one. Practice experience, however, would tend towards caution, as *Chapter 9* indicates.

Index

Crime, State and Citizen

A FIELD FULL OF FOLK

David Faulkner

Crime, State and Citizen is a wide-ranging and authoritative appraisal of the factors which sustain the fragile balance between effective government and individual rights and obligations in modern-day Britain. It is about: how Britain governs itself today; the rights and responsibilities of its citizens; the character of its public services and their relations with the state.

Writing at a time when issues such as the Rule of Law, human rights and cultural and human diversity are to the fore, David Faulkner examines these and similar questions by focusing on the politics and policies, and the professional standards and day-to-day arrangements, for dealing with crime and criminal justice - thereby touching on issues of immediate concern to Parliament, the Government, the courts, the other criminal justice services and individuals. He also explores the underlying aims and principles of justice, social inclusion, public safety (including matters of concern to victims of crime), accountability and legitimacy before suggesting how they should be applied and inescapable conflicts resolved.

David Faulkner is Senior Research Associate at the University of Oxford Centre for Criminological Research, where he writes about and teaches criminal justice, penology and government and public administration. He is Chair of the Howard League. In *Crime, State and Citizen* he also draws on a 30-year career working at the very heart of government – which included periods as Deputy Secretary of State in charge of the Criminal, Research and Statistical Departments of the Home Office, as Private Secretary to one Home Secretary (James Callaghan) and senior adviser to six others, and in the Cabinet Office. Over a period of 20 years he held direct responsibility for key aspects of the workings of criminal justice in the United Kingdom. He has contributed chapters to other works and published countless articles, but this is his first book. 360 pages. ISBN 1 872 870 98 8. £22.50 plus £2 p&p

With a Foreword by Lord Windlesham

01962 855567
www.watersidepress.co.uk

A key text from
Waterside Press